Author's Note

Astrology as a subject has survived thousands of years. Today it is emerging from a "dark period" of several centuries, during which its truths were scorned as mere superstitions as man's increasing scientific knowledge developed parallel with an increasing materialistic evaluation of life. During this period the charlatans and fortune-tellers debased and misinterpreted a great truth.

The profound—perhaps even astounding—truth about astrology is that through its basic formulae one can learn the intricate psychological structure of one's own being; trace the deep-rooted drives and motives for behaving as one does. Its value to parents, social welfare and probation officers, teachers, psychologists, the medical profession, in fact to all who seek truth and understanding of the human mind, is inestimable.

After over thirty years as an astrological consultant and teacher of astrology to students in over one hundred different countries, I have yet to meet anyone who, having put astrology to the test, has rejected the subject as nonsense.

Other Books by The Author

Teach Yourself Astrology
The Astrologer's Astronomical Handbook
How to Read the Ephemeris
How to Cast a Natal Chart

THE PLANETS
AND
HUMAN
BEHAVIOR

JEFF MAYO

CRCS PUBLICATIONS
Post Office Box 1460
Sebastopol, California 95472

Library of Congress Cataloging-in-Publication Data

Mayo, Jeff.
   The planets and human behaviour.

   Includes index.
   1. Astrology and psychology. 2. Planets--Miscellanea.
I. Title.
BF1729.P8M38 1985   133.5'3   85-22367
ISBN 0-916360-27-X

FIRST U.S.A. EDITION—Originally published in Great Britain
by L. N. Fowler, Ltd.
INTERNATIONAL STANDARD BOOK NUMBER: 0-916360-27-X
Published simultaneously in the United States and Canada by:
CRCS Publications
Distributed in the United States and Canada by
CRCS Publications
Cover Design: Image & lettering both by Rebecca Wilson

If the human psyche is anything, it must be of unimaginable complexity and diversity, so that it cannot possibly be approached through a mere psychology of instinct. I can only gaze with wonder and awe at the depths and heights of our psychic nature. Its non-spatial universe conceals an untold abundance of images which have accumulated over millions of years of living development and become fixed in the organism. My consciousness is like an eye that penetrates to the most distant spaces, yet it is the psychic non-ego that fills them with non-spatial images. And these images are not pale shadows, but tremendously powerful psychic factors. . . . Beside this picture I would like to place the spectacle of the starry heavens at night, for the only equivalent of the universe within is the universe without; and just as I reach this world through the medium of the body, so I reach that world through the medium of the psyche.

Dr. Carl G. Jung: Freud and Psychoanalysis

Contents

Foreword

Man has now set foot on the Moon, and this new era of space travel creates for the human mind a fresh dimension in thought-experience and imagination. The potential for deeper physical exploration into previously inconceivably distant areas of the Solar System knows no bounds. Man is on the threshold of yet more thrilling ventures into his cosmic environment and his ceaseless pursuit of understanding his biological relationship with all natural phenomena.

Parallel with this tremendous scientific step forward into the universe beyond the Earth there is a significant and exciting increase in the study and analysis of man's *physiological* and *psychological* relationship with his environment. Inevitably, scientists and biologists are turning their attention to research that must ultimately lead to a clearer understanding of the subtle forces by which man lives and thinks, and through which he is related to the cosmos. The ancient non-scientific thinkers among our ancestors conceived man's relationship with God and the heavens in the axiom, "as above, so below"—the idea of man, the microcosm, as an epitome of the macrocosm or universe. Thus was astrology born.

Today, one of the most fascinating studies of cyclic activities and rhythmic behaviour responses in living things, from plants, insects, animals, to man himself, has confirmed that the cells of living organisms are *physiological clocks* or *biological clocks*. The internal clock implies a physiological measurement of time, enabling an organism to adapt itself to the spatial con-ditions and the timing order of its environment. These bio-rhythms can be synchronized to the geomagnetic field and the Earth's rotation, and to the lunar and solar cycles. However, man's biological and cellular orientations to rhythms in his cosmic and geomagnetic environment is not confined to that of a timing mechanism, but seems to be linked also with psychological processes.

Astrology, as the interpretation of solar, lunar, and planetary inter-relationships in terms of life-processes, is being applied daily by large numbers of researchers in various scientific fields, though their work is obviously not classified under the name of "astrology". But it is encouraging to the dedicated astrological researcher and student to read the reports of scientific bodies. For instance, in *Hospital Focus*, published 15 February 1965 by Knoll Pharmaceutical Company of Orange, New Jersey, it is stated that "the heavenly bodies have distinguishable effects on biological materials", and "questions arise with rather prickling significance for epistemology. If it is verified that human processes are affected by the magnetic field interactions among celestial bodies, and if the Babylonians and Harappans knew nothing at all [sic] about wave mechanics or the solid state, how were they able to conceive of astrology?" Dr. L. J. Ravitz, a psychiatrist, wrote in the July 1952 Connecticut State Medical Journal of his work in regard to electromagnetic fields in human beings, "This study strongly suggests that certain and probably all living organisms are acted upon by cosmic forces transcending local environments, but characteristic of the ordered Universe of which we are all unquestionably a part."

This present book is intended as a very humble contribution to the study and theory of solar, lunar, and planetary correlations with human behaviour. For more than a dozen years I have been interested in Dr. Carl Jung's analytical psychology theories and the significant way in which many of these can be correlated with certain astrological factors and concepts. But, however much I may personally believe that astrological factors can be shown to correlate with Jung's theories of the human psyche, I would wish to see a great deal of statistical research undertaken in this field of psychological study.

Readers who may find references to Jungian psychology rather difficult to absorb, will find much else of interest. Varied traditional theories regards matters connected with the planets (e.g. certain anatomical features and physical disorders, vegetation, colours, metals and minerals) are included mainly for their curiosity value, and certainly not for any established validity. *Astronomical* data has purposely been omitted as this can be referred to in my *The Astrologer's Astronomical Handbook*,[1] and I have also purposely omitted the correlation of *physical characteristics* with the planets, as a title devoted entirely to this side of astrology is planned for future inclusion in this Handbook series.

The Sun and the Moon may for convenience be referred to in the text as "planets" when it is necessary to speak of the Sun, Moon and the eight actual planets of the Solar System (excluding our planet Earth) together.

The most commonly accepted symbols, as used in this book, are:

⊙ Sun
☽ Moon
☿ Mercury
♀ Venus
♂ Mars
♃ Jupiter
♄ Saturn
♅ Uranus
♆ Neptune
♇ Pluto

NOTE

1. Publisher: L. N. Fowler & Co. Ltd., London, 1965.

1 *From Galaxies to Human Cells*

Common to All Humanity

If the reader of this book is not a student of astrology he or she may well ask, "What is the basic theory behind astrology, that one should assume that the planets have got anything to do with human behaviour?" A perfectly logical question, especially when one considers the vast distances separating our own planet from the other bodies in the Solar System.

Briefly, the astrological theory is that the positions of the Sun, Moon, and the eight planets at the moment of a child's birth, and relative to the point on the surface of the Earth where birth occurs, correlate with potential behaviour-patterns and dominant drives and desires in that child. These planetary positions are plotted in the child's birth-chart according to the time and place of birth. When the *exact* time of this event is known, the chart-pattern will describe a significantly individual psychological pattern unique for that child and for *any other* child who is also born at that identical moment in time and approximately the same point (place, town) in space.

Other babies born on that same day, but at different times and in different places throughout the world, will also have those same planets plotted in their birth-charts. But because of the differences in time and location the relationship between the planets and other vitally important areas of the birth-chart will vary—giving significant differences in the basic psychological pattern innate in each child.

And also other babies born in other years—at any time or place one may care to think of—will have these same planets plotted in their respective birth-charts, if these charts could be known.

This implies a very important fact: the Sun, the Moon and the eight planets used in astrology are factors *common to all humanity*. The basic meanings, the basic principles, in terms of human behaviour, which astrologers attribute to each planet, are to be found within each human being.

Yet no two babies can ever be identical or could ever be expected to develop into the same adult person. Not even twins born only minutes apart. Parent-child relationship, childhood environment and circumstances of upbringing and of events in the parental or foster home, and the continuous stream of changing external circumstances and pressures and stimuli throughout life, will tend to bring different opportunities for the development of the innate potentialities of behaviour and mental growth. Also, there must be the important hereditary factors to take into account, as well as that unpredictable, unknown factor of "spirit", the "divine spark"—call it what one may—within the individual human being, that will contribute to the choice of reaction to external life, to the measure of strength or weakness of will-power to meet the challenge of physical, psychological and environmental limitations. As an astrologer I have never claimed that the planetary positions at a given moment of birth must correlate with *all* there is to know about the person concerned. But the basic psychological framework, indicative of potential behaviour-patterns and limiting factors, will definitely be predictable according to the planetary pattern at birth, and its relationship to the ecliptic and to the birthplace.

Whatever the variations and contrasts may be of the unknown spiritual entity and hereditary factors which contribute to making each human being unique, and whatever each may encounter through parental and environmental influences, there will ever be that heritage common to all humanity: *man's constant, inseparable link with his cosmic environment.*

Man's Inseparable Link with Cosmos

When we speak of "man's constant, inseparable link with his cosmic environment" what exactly do we mean?

Our own planet Earth is a part of the Solar System. Our planet orbits the Sun and one full cycle takes about 365 days to complete. Man calls this measurement a "year". If it were not for the gravitational pull of the Sun, our planet would hurtle into "space" and ultimately disintegrate. Similarly, the other known planets within our Solar System endlessly orbit this planetary system's central source of energy, the Sun. But the Sun is not the only body capable of producing gravitational energy. Each planet has its own magnetic field and accordingly has a gravitational affect on every other planet. There is a continuous, harmonic, counter-balancing interplay of gravitational forces between every body in the Solar System. The Sun is the dominant source of reference, the all-powerful, vital integrating factor.

The Sun is the heart or nucleus of the Solar System. But the Sun with its system of planets is also revolving round a centre, the *galactic centre*, which is the heart or nucleus, the source of reference, within the galactic system. Our Sun is but one of one hundred thousand million stars which gravitate round the source of energy at the heart of the Galaxy or galactic system. On a clear dark night we may see the encircling edges of this awe-inspiring stellar system, in the form of the Milky Way—the glittering, luminous belt composed of millions of stars, and who knows how many millions of other solar systems similar to our own.

Circles within circles, cycles within cycles. The galactic system bounded by the Milky Way is one of ten thousand million galaxies in the *observable* universe. And beyond these stellar systems it is conceivable that the energy of cosmic life radiates from even larger all-embracing systems, *ad infinitum*.

"Life is one great energy-system. Within this energy-system are infinite aggregations of lesser energy-systems. Each is concerned with maintaining itself, yet is dependent upon its environment and other energy-systems, each giving and taking, creating and maintaining the vital equilibrium."[1]

And so we may think of the ancient Hermetic axiom, "as above, so below". Energy-systems in an ever-decreasing scale from galaxy to Solar System, from star to planet and to man, from man to atom and microscopic cell. Each energy-system may be seen as a separate cell, yet dependent upon and maintained by other cells, whether the cell is a galaxy, a star, a human being, or one of the billions of cells of which a man is formed. "The cell is a dynamic equilibrium. . . . From and to the world around it takes and gives energy. It is an eddy in a stream of energy."[2]

Even each microscopically small cell in the human body possesses its own nucleus, which may be regarded as the very heart of its being. The nucleus exercises control over all the cell's activities, which include a hundred different chemical processes that are occurring simultaneously. "The cell represents the body in miniature. It may be looked upon as a working model in which we can study on a smaller scale the activities that take place in the body as a whole."[3]

Incredibly, perhaps, we may try to visualize a single human cell creating by its dynamic, restless activity an "eddy in a stream of energy" as it goes through the functions of digestion, absorption, metabolism, excretion, respiration and reproduction. Muscle-cells, nerve-cells, brain-cells, each has its own characteristic behaviour and vital role in the maintainence and equilibrium of the whole organism. Each cell is an organized energy-system centred upon itself, and yet functioning interdependently with other energy-systems. And when we classify our own self as a cell within the organism of the human race, it is perhaps easier to think of our own thoughts and behaviour creating an "eddy in a stream of energy".

It is but one step beyond man to reach into the cosmos of which our planet and the other bodies in the Solar System are separate and yet interdependent cells forming a vaster organism.

Thus may we profitably reflect on a basic principle of life, the *pattern* of which links each microscopic human cell with the planets and billions of distant stellar systems: *each cell is an organized life-system, energy-system, centred upon itself, and yet functioning interdependently with other energy-systems.* This is what we mean when we speak of "man's constant, inseparable link with his cosmic environment".

Planet–Man Correlation: Synchronistic?

Man is not an isolated, self-contained being. He is dependent upon his immediate environment for sustenance and equilibrium of being; upon other life-forms and forces and energy-systems that are present on the face of the Earth and in the atmosphere enveloping the Earth. Likewise this planet Earth interacts interdependently with other bodies in the Solar System, and is not a separated sphere falling through cosmic space without purpose and immune to the influencing forces produced by the Sun and Moon and other planets. We know that the billions of human cells are affected not only by the internal physiological life-functions of man, but also by incoming external environmental forces. "Without the ability to react readily to external influences, life would be impossible. The external dialogue between man and space seems to be indispensable to our survival."[4] We have seen that our own planet is affected by its cosmic environment, and inevitably this huge, spinning mass of organic and inorganic matter is subject to internal processes necessary for maintaining its existence and structural identity and its purpose as a part of the Whole scheme of cosmic life. Cells within cells. Stellar system, planet, man, human cell: each perhaps a replica of an original blue-print design for re-creating and maintaining life.

It may be so, that streams of life-promoting and life-sustaining energy enters man from beyond Earth. From the Sun, the Moon, the other planets, and even in infinitesimal quantities from distant galaxies. Feeding and stimulating his billions of cells, particularly through the fluids within every particle of his body. "Scientists have begun to accept the idea, until recently unbelievable, that the influences of space penetrate everywhere . . . affecting all organisms. . . ."[5] What was once a huge joke at the astrologers' expense is now regarded as more than just a theory. "Science does teach us that the whole universe is reflected in a drop of water, that the cosmic rhythms are necessary to the survival of life. Thus we begin to see that our bodies are in fact tied with invisible strings to the cosmos, as was dimly realized in the past."[6]

And so the astrologers are no longer alone when they speak of "planetary influences". As was known to be inevitable, a matter of time, the astrologers have been joined by the scientists and the biologists. But in speaking of an inseparable, an inextricable, link between man and his cosmic environment in terms of physical forces, created and forged in the single impulse that was the origin of life, even though man in his earliest organic form appeared billions of years after the stellar structures were designed, we must understand the essential link to be possibly one of *synchronization*.

The planets *did not create* man and the other forms of terrestrial life. The idea, the potentiality, for man to develop into his existing form of physical and psychic properties, would always have been present. The planets cannot, therefore, be said to *cause* a man to be born with predictable potentialities for behaviour. The correlation between planets and man is believed to be *synchronistic*. At any given moment the life-principle of a planet and the pattern formed by interplanetary gravitational fields correspond to a predictable growth-formation and a potential psychological pattern of behaviour in man.

That a planet can *influence* a man through his highly sensitive living substance is known to be true in the physical sense. But the scientists have yet to prove to their own satisfaction that the planets *do* influence man's behaviour and psychological make-up to the extent claimed by astrologers. This is understandable. The astrologers, too, would be interested to have positive scientific and statistical proof of the validity of astrological theories.

Yet whatever evidence may be forthcoming to indicate that each planet, and a combination of two or more planets when angularly related in varied ways, do have definite affects on man's psychological structure and activities, it is highly probable that the synchronistic principle will be accepted as the reason for the correspondence between planetary inter-relationships and human behaviour. It will be understood that the planets do not create or control terrestrial and human life, but that there could be a *common cause* for the synchronized and inter-related existence of both. This is one of the important keys to the understanding of astrology. It is also one of the most exciting concepts about man and the universe.

NOTES

1. Jeff Mayo: *Teach Yourself Astrology*, p. 15 (The English Universities Press Ltd.).
2. Kenneth Walker: *Human Physiology*, p. 9 (Pelican Books).
3. Sir Charles Sherrington: *Man On His Nature*, p. 81 (Pelican Books).
4. Michel Gauquelin: *The Cosmic Clocks*, p. 223 (Henry Regnery Co., Chicago).
5. *Ibid.*, pp. 144–5.
6. *Ibid.*, p. 226.

2 From God-Force to Magnetic Fields

From what has been said in the previous chapter, we may justifiably say that *man exists because of his cosmic environment.* Man, the Earth, the Sun and Moon, and the eight other known planets of the Solar System, appear to participate in the mathematically calculable functions of a vast energy-system.

Leaving aside the existing, and largely irrational, prejudices of the bulk of scientists against astrology, the fully-trained and knowledgeable astrologer can confidently state that the basic theories of his subject are valid. The Sun, Moon and planets can be shown to correlate with and symbolize *basic life-principles or functions* in man.

But the planets have not always been interpreted in quite this form.

Planetary Gods

Primitive man lived in a world where death could lurk behind any tree or rock. We can only imagine what kind of an existence this must have been, where the emotion of *fear* would have been a dominant reaction of his life by day and by night. In the light of his dimly awakening consciousness animate and inanimate objects alike were worshipped. Everything possessed a spirit of its own. He associated particular objects with the many gods whom he felt to dominate and control his life, and to whom, perhaps, he must offer sacrifices of appeasement when things were not going right.

We may say, therefore, that it is understandable that such magnificent and impossible-to-be-touched objects in the heavens as the stars, glittering forth from the otherwise fearful darkness of the all-enveloping night, should have been worshipped with the deepest awe. Ultimately, through careful observation and recording of the nightly cyclic return of the patterns formed by groups of stars, men recognized that certain "stars" did not remain in a fixed position relative to the other stars. They followed curved paths of their own apparent choosing. These free-moving bodies came to be known as the "wandering stars". Later, they were seen not to be stars at all, but planets, satellites of the great luminary, the Sun.

For primitive man these "wandering stars" would seem to move by their own volition, and who can say what inner sense prompted or compelled these early observers to associate the planets with the power and qualities of *particular* gods? We would be foolish to attach no significance to this association of particular gods with the "wandering stars" or planets, and very naïve to merely read with amusement of the special qualities attributed to these deities. This early, groping stage in man's identification of a god-force outside himself with potential qualities within himself, was no chance happening. This may be seen as a natural stage of awakening consciousness, an impulse derived from man's elementary experiences of living, forged and projected by his own psychic energies from within the dark unconscious depths of his being.

The development of astrology has been a continuous process extending over thousands of years. The present-day astrological-consultant, who has received a sound training in calculatory and interpretational theory and is conversant with the astronomical framework upon which these theories are based, practises a complex and intellectually-stimulating subject which is far removed from the star-worship and mystical practices and fortune-telling of his ancestral priest-astrologers.

But let us not underestimate the significance of the earliest attempts by man to understand the deep feelings he must have experienced through his observation of the stars and other celestial bodies. "What the early priest-astrologers perceived in the planetary patterns as the influence of their gods, resident in these planets, the astrological-consultant associates with impulses and drives rooted in the unconscious mind of his client, reflected in disposition, emotional response, general behaviour. The stream of thought has spanned the centuries unbroken from its source in antiquity, and with time and distance its course is broader and its banks more fertile with the growth of deeper understanding."[1]

For those of us who have practised astrology for years, and have daily seen the evidence of planetary symbology manifesting in the behaviour of our closest associates and our clients, the existence of astrology as a means of interpreting human psychology is as natural a feature of the evolution of mankind as the need for religion, the need to understand oneself in relation to the objects and forces of our environment that has led to astonishing scientific discoveries and the stepping of man on to the Moon.

If we think of astrology as a system of interpreting planetary inter-relationships in terms of human behaviour and activities, we may say that astrology had no clearly defined beginning. As a subject it was no more "invented" by any one man or group of men than were the varied languages of mankind. The need to communicate man with man produced significant oral sounds and determined the *evolution* of the symbols of language, the alphabet. The need to communicate and relate his deepest feelings, emotions, imaginings, excitement and fears to a visible deity or deities depicted by primitive man in the awe-inspiring and recurring phenomena of Sun, Moon, stars and planets, determined the *evolution* of astrology.

The earliest traces of astrological knowledge go back thousands of years and are found among the Chaldeans and Sumerians. There seems to have been no country or early form of civilized community where astrology was not developed. As has already been shown, one of the initial impulses in these early communities was to attribute to each planet a particular deity and name. The planet in which a particular deity was believed to dwell would be associated with the characteristics and powers possessed by the deity. The ceaseless activity of the celestially-residing gods was evident in the constantly changing appearance of the heavens and movements of the planets, and it was believed that this was reflected in the ever-changing happenings on earth due to the influence of these divine beings.

Whether we read the present-day textbooks on astrology, or the astrological writings of fifty or a hundred years ago, or study the historical records of the ancient priest-astrologers' theories on the subject, we arrive at the same conclusion: the Sun, Moon and planets are believed to influence or to correlate in predictable ways with patterns of human behaviour and affairs.

Planetary Magnetic Fields

Until recent times few astrologers seemed to be interested in trying to find out *how* the planets could possibly be related to human psychology. It was sufficient for most to know that this correlation *does* exist. But now, in my opinion, we *need* to know just how this can occur. And I am convinced that in the years ahead the subtle, true facts of man's inseparable relationship with the planets and with the infinite range of influences entering his environment from cosmic 'space' will be discovered. The receptivity of man's physical and psychic structure and organism to external influences cannot be confined to his few known senses. It is conceivable that the human body and its psychic counterpart are sensitive in as yet unknown ways to cosmic forces.

The perfectly organized life-promoting and life-sustaining activities of each of the billions of microscopic human cells could be a clue to the existence of man's vital link with his Earth and cosmic environments. "However primitive, all cells perceive cosmic forces and respond to them through mechanisms not yet understood."[2]

It is a recognized fact that a deficiency or an excess of particular chemicals in the body, an inharmonious functioning of the endocrine system, will create abnormal behavioural reactions in an individual. For instance, the parathyroids regulate the metabolism of calcium and phosphorus, and when the parathyroids are functioning inadequately and there is a deficiency of calcium and phosphorus in the blood, the individual becomes pathologically nervous, oversensitive, irritable. We all know the uplifting psychological affect of a spell of warm sunshine after a depressing period of rain and darkening clouds. But is this cheering, vitalizing affect due *only* to the sight of the brightening sunshine and the physical sensation of increased warmth?

The magnetic activity of the Sun affects the Earth's own

magnetic field and variations in terrestrial magnetism in turn affect man's own magnetic force field. A New York scientist, Dr. Robert O. Becker, wrote: "Subtle changes in the intensity of the geomagnetic field may affect the nervous system by altering the body's own electromagnetic field."[3] The studies of other scientists have shown that increased sunspot activity runs parallel with an abnormal increase of some components of blood, lymphocytes (white cells) in particular. As for the affects of the Moon, from ancient times the increased excitement of the emotionally disturbed and lunatics (*lunar*: Moon) has been noted at times of Full Moon. The female menstrual cycle, and in recent years other biological activities, have been significantly correlated with the lunar phases.

A distant planet's supposed range of disturbing influence on the terrestrial magnetic field is said to be extremely weak compared to the effects of the Sun and Moon. But why should this lesser affect be assumed to be of no significance?

Which brings us to the critical question: is the cause of the planets' correlation with human behavioural patterns and temperamental types a solely physical phenomenon? Or is it that of a common cause, as previously suggested, for the inter-related existence of man and planet, in terms of a synchronistic principle?

It could be a necessary combination of both. Inter-related planetary patterns synchronize predictably with human behavioural patterns, in the sense that the planets provide necessary physical stimuli followed sequentially by subtle and complex chemical and other minute changes within the fluids and cells of the human body—which could have resultant affects on the psyche, or provide the appropriate conditioning for potential psychological traits to manifest.

In my *Teach Yourself Astrology*[4] I wrote: "The present-day trained astrologer does not think in terms of light-rays or *influences* coming direct from each planet in the way that heat-rays from the Sun on a summer's afternoon stimulate the physical sensation of warmth and a feeling of well-being. The essential correspondence is one of space–time *synchronization*."

In the light of recent studies published by scientists I am personally happy to revise my opinion regarding planetary *influences.* Probably like most other serious students of astrology I have always *wanted* to believe and have it scientifically confirmed that the human psyche is directly influenced through its physical media by solar, lunar and other cosmic forces. What had always been impossible to accept was the manner in which so many astrological writers invariably used the term "influenced", as though it were the direct expression of the physical planet possessed with characteristics, and human vices and virtues. For instance, how could one possibly expect to hold the interest of an intelligently enquiring scientist by quoting Max Heindel and "the unrestrained passionate rays of Mars and the Moon".[5]

When one is conversant with astrological terminology one knows what Heindel meant. He is indicating that when Mars and Moon are shown to be in conjunction or afflicted in a birth-chart there is likely to be a tendency for passionate sexual forms of expression. Whether this potential trait is evident or not will depend on the relation that is shown between Mars–Moon and the chart-pattern as a whole. Thus, in extreme cases, and when other chart factors tend to activate the Mars–Moon combination, this could be a vital clue for the understanding of that person's bouts of "unrestrained passionate behaviour".

It is just unfortunate that for such a long time so many astrological writers have continued to interpret the correlated psychological affects of the planets as though *the planets themselves* also possess these human traits. This way of thinking of the planetary influences has been largely a blind acceptance of traditional astrological thought-patterns, which were formulated many centuries ago when each planet was indeed felt to be the visible expression of a destiny-controlling deity.

We find Llewellyn George saying that "Venus is termed a feminine planet. . . . Her influence is expressed as generous, kind, good-humoured and loving. She is considered benefic, warm, moist and fruitful."[6] And then Joan Rodgers tells us that "Mars is direct, blunt and brutal; he does not think of others. He is out to gratify his own desire to assert himself at all costs".[7] Of Uranus, Alan Leo reminds us that "All metaphysical thought and advanced views find in him a leader; in fact his influence is so marked and romantic, that once it is felt it never can be forgotten. He waits to afflict, but out of his evil good always comes."[8]

The above examples are not quoted because there is any intention of disparaging these three astrologers' writings. These have been chosen at random, and any reader could find similar examples of *personification* of the planets given in many other astrological books by different authors.

The reason I have quoted examples of this type of writing, in which a planet is personified, and apparently attributed with human characteristics, is to show what I have always felt to be a misleading form of interpretation. Obviously these three writers from whom I have quoted did not really mean that the actual planet Venus is "good-humoured and fruitful", or that Mars can in fact seek to "gratify his own desire and be brutal", or that the planet Uranus is capable of behaving "romantically". It is just their way of saying that these three planets *represent* in astrological terms those particular human traits.

You may say, as long as we know what is meant, where is the harm? where is it misleading? This method of interpreting the planets can be misleading for two main reasons. Firstly, it is of course incorrect in this twentieth century to personify a planet, and to the uninformed or sceptics this method of interpretation only continues to depict astrology as at best a subject full of mysticism and black magic mumbo-jumbo and, at worst, a subject that must be utter nonsense if a planet is said to behave like a human being. Secondly, and most important of all, this manner of talking about the planets can have no bearing whatsoever on the probable true correlation between planet and man. It gives a wrong impression of what we surely wish to be thought of as planetary *influences*. The implication in these writings is not only of a direct planetary influence, but that every shade and quality of behaviour the human animal is capable of expressing is determined by one planet or the other due to these heavenly bodies being the *originators* of these traits.

This is an idea, of course, that we cannot accept. The planets are not the prime creators of the human form and psyche. The origins of the human race are likely to be most deeply rooted in the origins of the planet Earth; in the evolutionary development of the substances forming the geophysical crust and the atmospheric environment. Here, within the organic and chemical substances of the Earth's mantle where it encounters the life-sustaining and life-protecting forces of atmosphere and geomagnetic field, man will have emerged and his present form been determined by the evolutionary design of a chain of biological processes unbroken for millions of years. It may eventually be found that the influence of the planets, though of tremendous and inevitable importance because of their inescapable link with man on a cosmic scale, provide a multitude of *potential variations* in human behaviour and temperament; and that the planet Earth to which man gravitates as a plant's roots to the soil, and certain biological factors inherited from the parents at the moment of conception, provide other vital ingredients which direct the subject's psychological development in distinctly characteristic directions.

NOTES

1. Jeff Mayo: *Teach Yourself Astrology*, p. 9 (The English Universities Press Ltd.).
2. Professor René Dubos, The Rockefeller University: *The Cell*, p. 6 (Time-Life Books Pocket Edition, 1969).
3. "Magnetic Man", *Newsweek*, 13 May 1963.
4. P. 2 (The English Universities Press Ltd., 1964).
5. *The Message of the Stars*, p. 37 (The Rosicrucian Fellowship, 1947).
6. *The A to Z Horoscope-Maker*, p. 43 (Llewellyn Publications, 1966).
7. *The Art of Astrology*, p. 115 (Herbert Jenkins, London, 1960).
8. *Practical Astrology*, p. 92 (Nichols & Co., London, 1909).

3 Symbols

The Sun's Symbol (☉)

The symbol for the sun is always shown as a circle with a dot in its centre.

Down through the ages astrologers have interpreted the *circle* as representative of wholeness, completeness, the life-giving principle or divine spirit. The *dot or point in the centre* is said to denote the reincarnated ego, the spark of divinity, the seed of potential perfection or godliness in the human spirit.

Alan Leo[1] wrote that the Sun's glyph symbolized "the one unity underlying all things. This Point in the Circle is the beginning of all that is to be, the unmanifested, absolute, permanent Centre, the unspoken Word from which all is to emanate." When Leo also suggested that the Sun was representative of the self he might have been foreseeing an important Jungian association of the self with the symbol of the circle, except that I can find no clear explanation as to what Leo meant by the self.

A. G. S. Norris[2] interprets the Sun's symbol very much in esoteric terms as "that of the Divine Life Essence focusing itself into matter as the energising principle of Force, Love and Wisdom, the point also representing the Ego bathing itself in the Divine Essence". By *Ego* Norris means "the true spiritual part of man". He continues, "As the point, in a rhythm of circles, gradually extends its radius of action towards the periphery and builds within the circle its own Star, so does the Ego's consciousness become merged in the Divine Consciousness symbolized by the circle." For those not initiated into esoteric terminology and patterns of thinking this kind of interpretation could be difficult to grasp, and impossible to apply in regard to his own potentialities in down-to-earth terms according to the Sun's position in his chart.

Margaret Hone[3] describes the solar symbol as "that of

Eternity, and of the power of spirit of primal motion, from whence all else issued and was created. It stands for the masculine principle of fatherhood."

Katherine Taylor Craig,[4] a writer of over fifty years ago, does not attempt to elaborate on occult themes regarding this symbolic circle and its central point, but suggests an easily understood analogy: "Its origin antedates history . . . the circle typifies the universe, the point the sun as the centre of our system."

The masculine principle or male generative life-force in nature, as the initial source of energy for creativity, is implied in many astrologers' interpretation of the symbol. As, for example, Marc Edmund Jones:[5] "Its symbol is the circle, suggesting infinite and undesignated potentiality, with the point or symbolization of manifestation placed at the centre to indicate its fundamentally focalizing activity. Here is self-assertion at simple root."

H. P. Blavatsky[6] indicates that the circle represents "cosmos in eternity" before the emanation of the Word (or Logos). "The point in the hitherto immaculate disk, space and eternity in dissolution, denotes the dawn of differentiation. It is the point in the mundane egg, the germ within the latter which will become the universe, the ALL. . . . The one circle is divine unity, from which all proceeds, whither all returns."

When studying the various interpretations of the Sun's symbol it is important to try to understand the central point or nucleus *in relation to* the circle.

A writer by the name of Mildred Kyle,[7] way back in 1917, has more or less summed up the essential idea within each of the previous quotes we have given. She wrote of the *circle*, "if taken alone, signifies the incomprehensible unity that underlies all manifestation. If applied to the whole vast universe, it stands for the Absolute, God unmanifested, all inclusive, without beginning or end. . . . When the circle is used in astrology it signifies the sun, which is the physical symbol of our Solar Logos, or God manifested in our solar system. When it is used for man it symbolizes the immortal spirit . . . always it symbolizes that which, like itself, has neither beginning nor end. . . . The circle without the dot represents life or spirit unmanifested;

with the dot it shows manifestation. All life begins to manifest from this central point. Wherever we see that point we know that it is a nucleus of life which will manifest as soon as it is given the proper conditions, as for instance, in the egg and all cellular formation."

We have seen the type of interpretation astrologers' give to the Sun's symbol. We may have our own very special variation to the generally accepted symbology. But there is one thing we are all likely to be agreed upon, and that is, the chosen symbol for the Sun could not possibly be more apt. The more we understand and practise astrology, the more significant—whether consciously or subconsciously—will that circle and its central point of focus be felt within ourselves each time we interpret the Sun in terms of human behaviour.

We cannot know when this particular and so very apt symbol came to be universally accepted as a symbol potent with meaning. The circle and dot combined are no doubt as old as astrology itself. The circle is older still. The creation of a circle is an archetypal experience mentally projected and given visible form. It was no chance matter that man's early psychic experience of the Sun's influence should be symbolized by the circle and dot.

Jung recognized the Sun's symbol as the classic symbol for the unity and divinity of the self, and as with many of Jung's conceptions of man's psychic structure and functions the self can be correlated with astrological factors. Jung sees the self as "not only the mid-point, but also the circumference that encloses consciousness and the unconscious; it is the centre of this psychic totality, as the ego is the centre of consciousness".[8] The self is the very core of the psyche, and yet it represents the whole man. It is the function which unites all the opposing elements in man and woman. "It marks the last station on the way of individuation, which Jung calls *self-realization*. Only when this mid-point is found and integrated can one speak of a 'whole man'."[9] Here we can see the close correlation between the traditional astrological symbology for the Sun, and this primordial archetypal process in man to achieve wholeness of being, self-integration, and conscious unity with his own true Self and with his environment and fellow creatures.

As the point, the nucleus, of the individual is contained within the centre of the circle which symbolizes the Sun, representing the archetypal process of self-realization and self-integration, so the centre of gravity of the individual, the very core of his psyche, is that which he must experience as his true self.

"Throughout the ages men have been intuitively aware of the existence of such an inner centre. The Greeks called it man's inner *daimon*; in Egypt it was expressed by the concept of the *Ba-soul*; and the Romans worshipped it as the 'genius' native to each individual. In more primitive societies it was often thought of as a protective spirit embodied within an animal or a fetish."[10]

And so the simplicity of the Sun's symbol, a dot within a circle, is really representative of a complex archetypal process of self-integration. This is the goal for realization that is symbolically implied. The self can be both the dot and the circle. It is a goal but also "a psychic category, experienceable as such; and if we abandon psychological language we might name it the 'central fire', our individual share in God, or the 'little spark' of Meister Eckhart. It is that focal point of our psyche in which God's image shows itself most plainly and the experience of which gives us the knowledge, as nothing else does, of the significance and nature of our likeness to God. It is the early Christian ideal of the Kingdom of God that 'is within you'. It is the ultimate experienceable in and of the psyche."[11]

Among the oldest religious symbols of mankind (the earliest known form being the sun wheel) is the *mandala*. It is found throughout the world among all peoples and in all cultures, even in sand-paintings, as among the Pueblo Indians. It was even to be found in paleolithic times. Mandala is a Sanskrit word meaning a circle, more especially a ritual or magic circle. The unique symbolism of the mandalas exhibits everywhere the same rules and regularity of arrangement, which is the reference of the elements, arranged in a circle or square, to a central point, by which "wholeness" is meant to be symbolized. Jung made a profound study of these symbols for fourteen years before he ventured on their interpretation. The mandalas used in Eastern ceremonial are of great significance because their centres usually contain one of the highest religious figures—perhaps Shiva or the Buddha, or one of the great Mahayana teachers. In Tantric yoga, mandalas were chosen as instruments of contemplation. Jung has shown that the mandalas belong to a most important domain of psychological experience. They signify a psychic centre of the personality, a psychological expression or primordial image of the totality of the self. Jung calls the mandala the *unifying symbol* and it usually appears in dreams or intuitively and is an essential feature in the process of individuation. The emergence of these mandala-symbols can have a remarkable effect, and it "leads as a rule to the solution of various psychic complications and a freeing of the inner personality from its emotional and conceptual confusions and disorders. Thereby a unity of being is produced that can rightly be termed a rebirth of man on a transcendental plane."[12]

I have mentioned the mandalas because of their extremely significant association with the Sun's symbol, and their undoubted confirmation of the process of self-integration, the unification of psychic opposites, symbolized by the Sun's glyph and represented for each one of us by the Sun in our individual birth-chart. Significantly, too, the birth-chart enclosed within the symbolic circle, is a mandala-symbol.

It is of much importance that the student of astrology understands the symbology of the circle and its central point, and their significance in terms of a realistic psychological interpretation of the Sun in astrology. The circle is a symbol of the self. "It expresses the totality of the psyche in all its aspects, including the relationship between man and the whole of nature. Whether the symbol of the circle appears in primitive sun worship or modern religion, in myths or dreams, in the mandalas drawn by Tibetan monks, in the ground plans of cities, or in the spherical concepts of early astronomers, it always points to the single most vital aspect of life—its ultimate wholeness."[13]

The Moon's Symbol (☽)

The symbol for the Moon is, in a sense, that of a half-circle. But it is drawn in two curved lines which correctly depict the *crescent* Moon as we can see it in the sky when the Moon is midway between New Moon (Moon conjunction Sun) and

First Quarter (Moon square Sun). A very few of the older text-books illustrate the Moon's symbol thus (☾). There seems no point in reversing the commonly accepted symbol in this way. The most apt glyph (☽) symbolizes the Moon as it begins a new cycle in relation to the Sun as seen from the Earth; whereas the reversed glyph (☾) symbolizes the Moon as it approaches the completion of a cycle—the crescent Moon between Last Quarter and New Moon.

Traditionally and esoterically astrologers describe the half-circle as symbolizing the *soul*, distinct from the circle that represents the immortal spark of *spirit* within man. The half-circle has also been associated with *mind*. Unfortunately, writers tend either to disagree as to exactly what they mean by "soul" and "mind", or they never bother to define these. Eso-tericists usually agree on one aspect of "soul", that this is also the "desire or emotional nature in man". It is to be assumed that "mind" refers to "mentality" or "mental process".

Another term associated with the Moon and its half-circle symbol, and in most cases loosely applied—by this I mean "inadequately defined"—is *personality*. A. G. S. Norris broadly defines personality as the "transitory" aspect of man. Vivian Robson sees the rapid physical motion of the Moon in its orbit of the Earth as indicative of the many and fluctuating changes that take place in the personality or "outer nature" of man.

Perhaps the American astrologer and occultist, Marc Edmund Jones, summed up the essence of what most other astrological writers infer by "soul" and "personality" when he wrote: "The crescent, or the half-circle . . . of the increasing Moon, is a character for soul in its simple form, i.e. that which by nature is part spirit and part spiritually incomplete, hence under necessity to fulfil itself."[14]

We may say then, in traditional terms, that the circle in its completeness symbolizes immortal spirit. The half-circle, being an incomplete circle, most aptly seems to represent evolving human spirit seeking completeness, wholeness of being.

Psychologists vary in their definitions of *personality*. I find Jung's concepts for both personality and *persona* ideally descriptive of these two important aspects of the human psyche. But I would not make any special symbolical connection between Jung's personality or persona and the half-circle. The most apt connections psychologically with the half-circle should be the *soul* (see page 142) and the *mind* (see page 137) as defined in Jungian psychology.

The *soul* is an inner personality, which is *complementary* to the outer personality or *persona*. The persona exists for reasons of adaptation to and the requirements of a man's environment. The persona is an "outer attitude" exclusively concerned with the relation to the object outside of man. Whereas the soul (or *anima* for a man, *animus* for a woman) is an "inner attitude", the inner personality, or the manner of one's behaviour towards the inner psychic processes and the vague, emotional stirrings of the unconscious. The soul contains those general human qualities of suggestibility and weakness which are wholly lacking in the outer conscious attitude or persona. *Mind* is *conscious* psychological activity, the expression of intelligence. And perhaps it can be said it is that which manifests itself in thought, in conscious awareness to feeling and desire, as that something which registers experience and motivates choice of behaviour.

The psychological functions most significantly associated with the Moon would appear to be those attributed to the Jungian *soul*, and in lesser part to the *conscious mind*. Mostly the other concepts of soul suggested by various astrological writers tend to be too vague to be acceptable. This is *not* to say that the Moon alone is associated with the soul and mind.

But I would freely admit that it is difficult as yet to understand how the half-circle can be employed in the Moon's glyph as symbolizing the soul, and in part the mind, whilst also appearing as a part of Mercury's glyph, where the function of mind is most decidedly that which is symbolized.

It must be significant that the Moon's symbol does not contain the *cross*—the symbol for *matter* or material conditions. This implies the emphasis on emotional and mental processes associated with the Moon factor in a birth-chart. Matter, earth, the physical form, imply solidity, a static condition, a distinct or concrete shape. Whereas the processes connected with the Moon are rhythmic ebb and flow, fluidity, constant changeability, as the ceaseless movement and swirl of ocean water and the ever-changing patterns of air currents and masses, and emotional and mental action-reaction.

Mercury's Symbol (☿)

In Mercury's glyph we have the three basic symbols, the circle, the half-circle, and the cross. "The half-circle (human spirit or mind) poised over the circle (divine spirit) and the cross (matter). Derived from the 'staff of Mercurius', the caduceus, consisting of two serpents around a rod, indicating the riddle of life. To understand this riddle requires mind and reason."[15] The half-circle atop the circle certainly appears to illustrate a head wearing a winged cap, as has been depicted of the Roman god Mercury.

The planet Mercury is a factor in the birth-chart associated essentially with "man the thinker". The two complementary opposites, spirit and matter, with added faculty of mind that has evolved through the incarnating of the human spirit into matter.

The significance of the circle being placed between the half-circle and the cross is suggested by Vivian Robson. "The semicircle over circle over cross, or the predominance of soul and spirit over matter and the blending of all three. The central position of the spirit denotes the alternation of emotion and matter through which the spirit is reached and to which it forms a point of balance."[16]

The mind (all *conscious* mental activity) is the dominating factor where the processes of the human psyche are associated with Mercury, as shown by the half-circle uppermost. In one sense we can say that matter (cross) is delegated to an inferior position at the base of Mercury's symbol. And yet in another and more logical sense it is to be understood that for the Mercurian communicative and co-ordinating processes to function and develop both soul and spirit must "work through" matter. Indeed, the physical has a vital role for the communication and transmission of experience, just as wires and valves and other more sophisticated material objects are necessary for transmitting radio and television sounds and pictures.

Venus's Symbol (♀)

In this symbol we see spirit (circle) supreme over matter or material conditions (cross). The half-circle (mind) is not present. This can be understood in the sense that Venus correlates with the human functions of evaluating experience through the *feelings*, as opposed to judgement through rational thought. Maybe the "spirit" aspect of Venus is most evident in terms of sensitiveness, creativeness, desire for beauty, harmony, love, and refinement in expression. In the glyph, *matter* (cross) is shown beneath spirit (circle), suggesting inferiority of matter. But don't let us underrate the importance of matter—of the flesh and material things in life—by thinking that the purpose of the Venus function within us is to help us to cast aside the "temptations" of fleshly desires and material attractions, and transmute the energies of desire for such earthly things into "spirituality". If it were not for our intricate *physical* means of transmitting sensory experiences through sight, touch, hearing, taste, smell via the complex *physical* brain structure, we could not possibly develop our faculty of feeling-evaluation, and learn to appreciate beauty and art, and be conscious of our fellow creatures and our love for them, and realize the desire to create new life or original forms of self-expression.

Through the feeling-function within the psyche, with which we associate Venus, man should learn to develop and use each feature of his body that can transmit sensation and sensory-awareness to experience, so that his feelings can be cultivated to the fullest degree of refinement and sensitivity. Through the necessary medium of physical body and earthly experience, this is the environment through which the individual will be enabled to achieve individuation, wholeness of being, symbolized by the circle over the cross.

In biology and medicine the Venus symbol is still the symbol for the feminine principle.

It has been said that this symbol also represents the "mirror of vanity" associated with the goddess Venus—the circle being the mirror, the cross its handle. It is also claimed to be the *Ankh*, the ansated cross or a phallic symbol of the Egyptians.

Mars' Symbol (♂)

In this symbol we have the circle (spirit) at the base of an arrow which is drawn pointing to the right at an angle of 45°.

Originally the symbol for Mars (♁) was the exact reverse to the symbol for Venus (♀). Matter (cross) is supreme over spirit.

The present symbol (♂) has been described as graphically depicting the shield (circle) and the spear of the Greek war-god Ares, who was identified with Mars the Roman war-lord, and with Mars the planet.

Marc Edmund Jones[17] states that the symbol has been "conventionalized with the cross of matter becoming a scorpion's sting. The symbolization dramatizes a self-assertion of the sort which demands that spirit be subordinated to matter, or that a practical employment be given to spiritual potentials."

The self-assertive, masculine implication of the Mars' symbol can also clearly be interpreted in sexual terms: "The *male sexual organ* is significantly resembled in erection in the Mars glyph, expressive of the phallus image that was once widely worshipped as a symbol of the generative power in nature."[18] This symbol is, of course, used in medicine and biology for the masculine principle.

The glyph symbolizes a function within both man and woman which is essentially physical and sensual in expression, of necessary masculine characteristics—objective, thrusting outwards and upwards towards a target. It is a symbol descriptive of energy-potential. I cannot agree with those writers who would have us believe that because the circle is beneath the cross (or arrow) this means that Mars is associated with bestiality, spirit is negatively suppressed by matter and lust for physical pleasures and materiality. It is true that a prominent and probably afflicted Mars is likely to be found in the chart of a person who is unpleasantly aggressive, or who is selfish and crude in achieving sexual gratification. But the real essence of the Mars principle that we associate with a function of the human psyche, is not that spirit has to be in any way *negatively suppressed* by this function. For man to achieve objectives for survival, and to successfully compete with his fellows, or to meet the challenges of attack or defence, human spirit must be *harnessed* to matter, to the flesh, to physical energy, to produce constructive forms of drive, initiative, self-assertion. The human spirit is, after all, of the physical body—the one is necessary for the evolution of the other. And both spirit and matter were created by the same source of life—whom men have called by the names of a thousand gods and devils.

Jupiter's Symbol (♃)

This symbol is composed of the half-circle (soul, mind) and the cross (matter). The half-circle is above the horizon or level of the cross, and yet is not completely above the whole cross. Traditionally this denotes that the human soul and mind must expand and develop new awareness and a higher consciousness beyond, yet out of, physical experience and the earthly environment.

Marc Edmund Jones[19] sees significance in the fact that the half-circle placed on the cross of matter is facing east or the Ascendant, if the horizontal bar of the cross is thought of as the Ascendant-Descendant axis of a birth-chart. He says, "thus emphasizing a type of self-assertion which is particularly eager to enter upon experience, or to give wholesouledly of itself in the act of being."

The theme of soul and emotional emphasis represented by the half-circle in Jupiter's symbol is generally to be found in the older textbooks. The half-circle being above the horizontal bar of the cross seems also to be accepted as indicative of Jupiter symbolically revealing that man bears within his psyche a function or potential ability to extend his consciousness and express his emotional nature unfettered by the seeming limitations of his physical body. Of Jupiter's symbol Alan Leo wrote that this portrayed "the soul expanding beyond matter, but retaining the material form".

Manly Palmer Hall[20] suggests that "the symbol is a conventionalization of an eagle with outstretched wings or as the letter Z of the Greek name Zeus, with a line through it to indicate an abbreviation".

If we also take into account that the circle (spirit) is not contained in this symbol it may be said that Jupiter represents a function within man's psyche through which his soul or inner personality, and his mind or conscious psychological activity, can be developed beyond yet out of physical and material experience and realities. To matter, or the raw materials of earthly existence, which man has inherited physically, he must inevitably adjust himself if he is to mature mentally and emotionally. The spirit of man presumably permeates every cell and nerve fibre of his being and is the motivating drive behind his soul reactions and mental activities. Therefore, even though the circle is absent from Jupiter's symbol, the psychic function represented by this planet has its spiritual connections. But the essential role of this function emphasizes the natural instinctive need for man to reach beyond his physical environment. Through deeper and wise participation in and understanding of mundane experiences. By learning to control his emotional drives through observance of just social laws and moral codes of behaviour, and yet preserve his natural right to develop his own unique nature if he is to realize ultimate wholeness of being or, as Jung would call this psychic process, individuation.

Saturn's Symbol (♄)

The half-circle (soul, mind) is below the horizontal bar of the cross (matter), implying that matter or physical limitations and boundaries have precedence over the inner expressions of soul and mind. Alan Leo's description is that the "concrete soul is limited by material conditions". "The soul at the nadir of matter" is Marc Edmund Jones' interpretation. In *Teach Yourself Astrology* I wrote that Saturn's glyph is "symbolic of the limitation and density of the physical, through which the human spirit, evolving as mind, must penetrate to make further growth and consciousness".

Apparently Saturn's symbol was originally identical to Jupiter's symbol if the latter were turned upside down. Certainly these two planets operate in so many ways as opposing functions within man's psychic structure. Jupiter is associated with *expansion*, Saturn with *restriction*. Through the Jupiter factor in his make-up man can express energy and desire *enthusiastically*, and realize the need for *progress* and *projection* of self and consciousness. Through the Saturn factor he expresses a *serious* and *disciplined* control of his energies and desires, and realizes the need for *stability*, *patience* and *self-restraint*.

Saturn's symbol has been identified with the scythe of the god Cronus, or Time (Father Time).

It is true that sorrow, bitter frustration, chronic sickness, miserliness, a cold and hard nature, can be associated with Saturn prominent and afflicted in the birth-chart. But this side of life and negative human behaviour has always been written about at the expense of the positive and constructive features. Saturn represents the *formative* principle in life. Saturn's symbol shows the cross of matter uppermost. This is excellent, since it symbolizes the necessary potential in man to adapt himself constructively and purposively to the material aspects in his life. Saturn indicates that in all men and women there is the potential builder, architect, thinker, disciplinarian, and master of mathematics and geometrical design. The "cross of matter", however hard it is to bear at times, is as necessary for the development of character as any other human function connected symbolically with the planets.

Uranus's Symbol (♅)

It is said that this symbol originated from the initial letter "H" of William Herschel's name, the astronomer who discovered this planet. What is a far more interesting connection is the similarity between this symbol and the first type of television aerial, when we consider it was inevitable that television as a medium for producing images had to be associated with Uranus.

What can we make of this curious symbol? The cross (matter) stands over the circle (spirit), and the cross is between two vertical lines. Some astrologers curve these lines, thus) (, depicting two different aspects of the crescent Moon. Llewellyn George[21] has suggested that the symbol for Uranus is a combination of Mars (♂) and Moon) (symbols. He believes this shows that while spirit (○) is still working through material conditions it is completely controlled by mind.

Alan Leo interprets the symbol as indicating "individualized self-consciousness". Vivian Robson[22] wrote, "the symbol represents the life emerging from the spirit, passing through matter, and converging into onepointedness. It is the planet of individualization, and represents the will or spirit that is ever pressing forward through changing matter." For Marc Edmund Jones[23] "here is symbolization of self-assertion directed towards the illimitable, or of human life as newly manifest in some enlarged dimension of self-act". He suggests that the "pictograph" or glyph expresses powers beyond normal activity and capacity and is fundamentally phallic. It can be described as the "ideogram for male potency combined with a limiting or conditioning fence or ladder, thus representing the necessity for personal re-orientation in a greater reality".

Certainly this symbol appears somewhat like the original symbol for Mars, with the circle beneath the cross. The distinguishing features are the two vertical bars, or pair of crescent Moons. Uranus was discovered in 1781, which in terms of astrological history is relatively recent. Thus, with regard to the symbols for the three "recently" discovered planets, Uranus, Neptune and Pluto, these seem perhaps to have been chosen too fortuitously for one to feel confident that one's interpretation is correct. For Uranus, my suggestion is that here we have the three basic symbols, circle, cross, and half-circle. There must be the initiatory, assertive, thrusting, venturesome nature of Mars, the exertion of energy (spirit impulse) which is suggested by the circle beneath the cross of material conditions. The two half-circles which are now shown as vertical lines enclose the cross. These imply the necessary involvement of mind and soul for this human faculty to develop and fulfil itself. This would be true of much that we associate with Uranus. The soul, or inner personality, may well be the source or motivating impulse for sudden dramatic flashes of originality, anarchy, unconventional behaviour, perversion, inventiveness, and *deviation from the normal* attitude and thought-patterns of the outer personality.

Neptune's Symbol (Ψ)

Neptune's glyph would appear to be very aptly chosen as symbolic of the *trident* of the sea-god, Neptune. But the trident-like symbol used in this book and by the Faculty of Astrological Studies, which is the symbol most widely used nowadays, is not employed by all astrologers. In the U.S.A., for instance, we will often find Neptune represented by ♇ or ♇. The latter symbol, showing the small circle at its base, could all too easily be confused with the symbol for Uranus (♅) if carelessly drawn.

We will contain our interpretation of Neptune's symbol to Ψ. Here we have the half-circle, indicative of the mind or soul, over the cross, representing matter or material conditions. The half-circle over the cross can symbolize the mind (or, if we like, evolving human spirit) dominant over matter. This suggests that the psychic function in man symbolized by Neptune will be developed most naturally as conscious awareness to the need for the elevation of mind over matter. This is not suggesting that matter, or the necessary and inevitable involvement with material and earthly and fleshly things, must be evaluated as inferior to the so-called "spiritual" part of man. Indeed, spirit or soul could not exist "as man or woman" were it not for this vehicle of flesh. Because we may speak of the uppermost part of a planet's symbol "dominating" the lower part, this does not mean that the upper is superior to the lower. It must be true that spirit and matter are equal in the sense of being complementary, as dual aspects of evolving life. Just as male and female are complementary aspects of the life-force within living organisms, of equal value and necessity.

Marc Edmund Jones conjectures that the naming of this planet after the Latin deity of the sea, and presumably the choice of symbol naturally being the trident, is significant in that the god Neptune and his fellow deity, Poseidon, "suggested the source of all experience in the eternal roots or springs of being. This dramatized the form of self-assertion by which an individual distributes his total obligation to society, or is compelled to do so, whether or no. The symbol superficially is the god's trident. More basically it is also phallic, suggesting the operation of a deeper reference in human capability, or illimitable personal capacity, through a modified pictograph of the female power in nature."[24]

My personal preference is that the half-circle over the cross may be seen as mind evolving out of necessary experience within and of the physical form and its functions. As mind or consciousness develops there should be a natural orientation towards *refinement* of self-expression. An interesting connection is the traditional identification of Neptune, through its symbol, with the chalice of the Holy Grail legends.

Pluto's Symbol (♇)

Quite simply this symbol appears to be a monogram composed of the first two letters of Pluto. But it is also stated to derive from the initial letters of Percival Lowell, the astronomer whose exhaustive calculations of this planet's probable position led to its eventual discovery by the Lowell Observatory about fourteen years after his death.

The symbol most widely used up to the present time in the U.S.A. is ♀. Marc Edmund Jones has interpreted this symbol as "soul creating spirit out of matter". The circle of spirit is seen embraced by the half-circle of soul, while resting on the cross of matter.

Will a new symbol eventually be chosen for this planet, as we come to realize more about the function it symbolizes or corresponds to within the psychic structure of man? Perhaps. We cannot know for how long the early "astrologically-thinking" men and priests were aware of their inner relationship with the Sun, Moon, and five first-discovered planets before symbols were ascribed to each—designed no doubt by the archetypal forces which had in the first instance caused men's minds to *need* to believe in such a cosmic-human relationship. Maybe it took many centuries before the ultimate symbols were projected by man's inner experience of these archetypal forces and cosmic energy-patterns into his conscious mind, when certain inspired men, in diverse, unrelated countries, wrote down each symbol for all to see. Maybe, like the little girl who chose the name for the newly-discovered planet Pluto, the real symbol for Pluto will be registered—in much less than several centuries hence—in the mind of an inspired astrologer.

NOTES

1. *Art of Synthesis*, p. 28 (L. N. Fowler & Co. Ltd.).
2. *Transcendental Astrology*, p. 52 (Samuel Weiser & Co.).
3. *The Modern Textbook of Astrology*, p. 25 (L. N. Fowler & Co. Ltd.).
4. *Stars of Destiny*, p. 35 (Kegan Paul, Trench, Trubner & Co. Ltd.).
5. *Astrology: How and Why It Works*, p. 265 (David McKay, Philadelphia, 1945).

6. *Two Books of the Stanzas of Dzyan*, pp. 35-6 (The Theosophical Publishing House, India).
7. *A to Z Horoscope-Maker*, by Llewellyn George, pp. 541-2 (Llewellyn Publications).
8. *The Integration of the Personality*, p. 96.
9. *The Psychology of Jung*, by Jolan Jacobi, p. 118 (Routledge & Kegan Paul, Ltd., London).
10. M.-L. von Franz in: *Man and his Symbols*, by Carl G. Jung, p. 161 (Aldus Books Ltd.).
11. *The Psychology of Jung*, by Jolan Jacobi, p. 123 (Routledge & Kegan Paul, Ltd., London).
12. *Ibid.*, p. 132.
13. Aniela Jaffé, in *Man and his Symbols*, by Carl G. Jung, p. 240 (Aldus Books Ltd.).
14. *Astrology: How and Why It Works*, p. 267 (David McKay, Philadelphia).
15. *Teach Yourself Astrology*, by Jeff Mayo, p. 26 (The English Universities Press Ltd.).
16. *A Student's Text-Book of Astrology*, p. 179 (J. B. Lippincott Co., Philadelphia and London).
17. *Astrology: How and Why It Works*, pp. 269-70 (David McKay, Philadelphia, 1945).
18. *Teach Yourself Astrology*, by Jeff Mayo, p. 31 (The English Universities Press Ltd.).
19. *Astrology: How and Why It Works*, pp. 270-1 (David McKay, Philadelphia, 1945).
20. *Astrological Key Words* (David McKay, Philadelphia).
21. *A to Z Horoscope-Maker*, p. 547 (Llewellyn Publications).
22. *A Student's Textbook of Astrology*, p. 180 (J. B. Lippincott Co., Philadelphia & London).
23. *Astrology: How and Why It Works*, pp. 271-2 (David McKay, Philadelphia, 1945).
24. *Ibid.*, p. 272.

4   *Myths and Deities*

Modern man is inclined to disregard the myths and legends of his distant ancestors as sheer fantasies created by minds that were at a very primitive stage in development. He tends to view the personification of inanimate objects and of the cosmic bodies with equal amusement and derision.

To understand the very real emotional content that was the energy for creating the myths of the ancients, we have to realize that for primitive man the natural world and his immediate environment must have been experienced in a totally different form to the way you or I would react to the same phenomena. For primitive man nothing was inanimate. Natural phenomena would be conceived in terms of human experience. "The fundamental difference between the attitudes of modern and ancient man as regards the surrounding world is this: for modern, scientific man the phenomenal world is primarily an 'It'; for ancient—and also for primitive—man it is a 'Thou'."[1] The sudden stab of lightning, the moving shadow of a windblown tree, the jagged rock that hurts him as he stalks his prey, the fear-provoking vanishing of the hot, fiery Sun behind a black cloud, the appearance of the Moon above the horizon at night —these would be experienced as a personal confrontation with living things possessing human characteristics. For primitive man his experience of inanimate phenomena was a relationship as real and as purposeful as his relationship with his own flesh and blood kind.

Myths were not *invented* by primitive man but were a natural account of his *experience* of his involvement with his environment, and of his conflicts, triumphs, fears. His accepted participation in the life of nature and in the recurring cosmic events would be dramatized in his rituals and festivals.

The very names given to the Sun and the Moon and the planets, and the myths associated with these cosmic bodies,

derived from archetypal expressions of the collective unconscious. The myth has a creative function as a living cultural
force. Myths that seem only to explain natural events, such as
sunrise and sunset, birth and death, have a deeper and more
significant meaning, expressive of man's inner and emotional
experience of these phenomena. The same would seem to apply
to the choice of names and the human characteristics attributed
to the celestial bodies.

The contents of the collective unconscious are expressed and
revealed through the *archetypes*. Jung has shown that there are
as many archetypes as there are typical situations in life. The
Sun in astrology represents an archetypal form, as does the Moon
represent another archetypal form, and each planet also. Archetypes manifest as *patterns of emotional and mental behaviour in
man*. They are inherited patterns, common to all men everywhere
and at any time. Dependent on the individual's time and place
of birth, so will it be seen to which archetypal patterns he will
be most significantly predisposed, and the potential modes
of his reactions to the challenge or conflict of these patterns.

Examples of inherited archetypal patterns are evident in the
fact that throughout the ancient world among different tribes
and peoples the same *types* of gods were chosen. Gods of
Earth, Sky, Thunder, War, Fertility, Sea, and the inevitable
Sun-god and Moon-goddess. It is clear from these few examples
that in most primitive mythological systems essential features
of man's environment appear to be embodied in his gods. Yet
would it not be that environmental features provide a corresponding form with which man can project outside himself the
archetypal impulses which seek to direct his life from within?
The cause, or the need, for man to create order and purpose for
his life comes from within himself. Man's earliest conception of
the creation of life is that it should have taken the form of a
birth. The cosmos is created out of chaos. The primeval parents
common to most primitive mythological systems are the Earth
Mother and Sky Father. Around this basic idea a complicated
system of deities would be developed.

The Sun

It is far too simple an explanation, and possibly misleading, for it to be said that the Sun *had to* be chosen as the most powerful of celestial deities just because of its powerful influence in the physical sense, as giver of light, heat, creative energy, and as a natural time-keeper. There was always an archetype corresponding to the role of the Sun in man's life. Thus it was easy for the Sun to personify for man a great many of his deepest feelings, and the repetitive rising, culminating, and setting of this fiery orb, and its being "swallowed up" by the darkness of night only to emerge again each day victorious from its eternal battle with Darkness, is depicted in the great many forms the Sun assumes in mythic fancy.

"The Sun is personified and regarded as a Shepherd, a Warrior, an Archer, a Lance-Holder, a Hunter, a Giant, a Water-pourer, a Sailor, a Charioteer; or, again, as a Ram, a Goat, a Horse, a Lion, an Eagle, or a Fish."[2] Probably the most fancied role of the Sun is that of a Hero, depicted in his battles with the elemental forces of the Sky and with Darkness. It is natural that the personified activities of the Sun and the Moon should be found linked in various myths, in which they are sometimes referred to as the "original Twins", or the "Two Hostile Brethren". Essentially the Sun and the Moon are seen to be engaged in securing the preservation of Cosmic order, and yet they can also be antagonistic, as the "Lion and the Unicorn". In *The Migration of Symbols*, Count Goblet D'Alviella notes that "in the mythology of primitive nations the contest between the sky, or sun, and the clouds is frequently represented by a fight between an eagle and a serpent". And Robert Brown[3] continues this theme with, "Here we meet with the solar Snake-holder. The Lion, king of beasts, the Eagle, king of birds, the Dolphin, king of fishes, are all specially sacred to the solar hero, whose most familiar mythological opponent is Darkness, appearing either as Night, Storm-cloud or Eclipse. . . . With this are closely connected Cold and Winter, and Autumn, the season when the light begins to fade quickly and the cold increases. As light and warmth are, on the whole, far more pleasant than darkness and cold, so the opponent of the solar hero takes a monstrous and horrid form and is portrayed as a Dragon, huge Serpent, Scorpion."

In the Bible Christ is associated with the Sun, in Malachi 4:2,

"But unto you that fear my name shall the Sun of righteousness arise with healing in his wings. . . ." Whilst in Revelations 12:1 we find the Christian Church "clothed with the righteousness of Christ" is symbolized: "And there appeared a great wonder in heaven; a woman clothed with the sun, and the moon under her feet, and upon her head a crown of twelve stars."

The following are some of the deities who have been associated with the Sun.

Adonis, an ancient Greek Sun-god, lover of Venus. The Hebrew god *Tammuz* is said to be identified with Adonis.

Aesculapius, the virgin born Sun-god and saviour of the ancient Greeks, and god of medicine.

Amen-Ra, an ancient Sun-god. Creator and "Lord of the Heavens".

Ammon, a great Egyptian and Ethiopian Sun-god (*Amûn*), whom the Greeks identified with Zeus, and the Romans with Jupiter. He was shown with the head of a ram, or with ram's horns, and it was thought that Aries was the sign of the king of the gods.

Apollo, one of the great divinities of the Greeks. Various powers are ascribed to him and among these he is seen as a Sun-god. It is asserted that the Greeks would never have become what they were, without the worship of Apollo. The Romans became acquainted with this divinity through the Greeks.

Atum, an Egyptian Sun-god, so powerful that he was worshipped under several names and aspects. He was *Aten* as the solar disc, *Khepera* (*Kheper*) when he rose in the east, *Ra* at the meridian, and *Atmu* when he set. He was also known as *Horus*, and as this divinity he was also worshipped in Greece and at Rome. Ultimately, Atmu, Horus, and Ra merged into one deity, *Ra Harakhti*, the Great Creator. Probably Atum is sometimes written *Tum*, an Egyptian Sun-god who originated from the ocean.

Baal, a phallic deity and Sun-god mentioned in the Scriptures, worshipped by the Phoenicians and the Israelites. Baalism was the worship of the powers of generation practised by the Canaanite race. Their creed was that out of a self-existent chaotic deep sprang spontaneously the heavenly bodies and the Earth; that, from the procreative power of the Sun, acting upon the fertile womb of the Earth, all visible matter was produced. The word Baal means Master, Owner, Possessor. A variant of Baal was *Moloch*, a Sun-god who it is said represented the Sun in its destructive aspects. Worshipped by the Ammonites, the early Canaanites and neighbouring Semitic tribes, and by some of the peoples of North Africa. *Belus* is another name for Baal.

Balarama (or *Balaram*), a Hindu Sun-god.

Balder (or *Baldur*, *Baldr*), a Nordic Sun-god.

Barsav-Perseus, a Greek Sun-god.

Chemosh, a Sun-god worshipped by the Moabites, worshipped by Solomon (I Kings 11:7). Said to be identified with Apollo.

Danae (or *Danai*), ancient pagan Sun-god, son of Belus.

Dazhbog (or *Dazbog*, *Dajdbog*), a Russian Sun-god and god of wealth and success.

Dianus, the Greek god of light, represented by the Sun.

Dionysus, the Semetic and Hellenic solar Goat-god. Has been depicted wearing an ivy-wreath. The Corona Borealis is connected with the god, the traditional inventor of crowns. Ancient Greek god of wine, identified with the Roman *Bacchus*, bore the same name.

El, Sun-god of the Syrians and Semites. Same as *Il* and *Ra*.

El Belus, an Assyrian and Babylonian Sun-god. The Tower of Babel, probably as a phallic symbol, was erected for the worshipping of this deity.

Erythros, a Kreton Sun-god.

Gad, probable Sun-god of Canaanitish nations.

Gilgames, Euphratean and Semitic Sun-god, the hero who has a special labour in each month and each sign of the zodiac.

Helios, Grecian Sun-god, called *Sol* by the Romans. Described as the god who sees and hears everything. Same as *Helius* of the Egyptians.

Helius, an Egyptian Sun-god.

Herakles, Phoenician Sun-god, opponent of monsters. He is variously depicted with a lion's skin over his arm, a crab at his feet, and wearing a gleaming gold belt wrought with bears, boars, and lions.

Hercules, mighty pagan Sun-god, worshipped by many nations and under various names. Son of Zeus.

Hyperion, a primitive Grecian Sun-god, son of Uranus (Heaven) and Ge (Earth), and father of Helios (the Sun), Selene (the Moon), and Eos (the Dawn).

Indra, Hindu god of the firmament and of rain and battle as well as a Sun-god. In India this solar god was styled "the Ram irradiating the firmament", which indicates that the association of the ram with Sun-gods was an idea arising naturally in the mind of man and was found in widely separated countries, and was not specially Indian, Akkadian, Egyptian or Aryan.

Inti, the Incan Sun-god.

Itzamna, Mayan Sun-god, later displaced by *Kukulkan*.

Llew Llaw Gyffes, an ancient British Sun-god.

Marduk-Merodach, ancient Babylonian Sun-god, who was responsible for the founding of the Zodiac. Earlier identified with Jupiter.

Mendes, ancient Egyptian Sun-god, worshipped in the form of a goat.

Mithras (*Mithra*), the god of Light and Wisdom among the Persians. At first a Sun-worship, it became modified by syncretism. He is the light and not the Sun; the Sun is his chariot, or rather his charioteer. His worship became very widespread. *Mithra* was the Sun-god in the mythology of the Brahmanic Dharma in India, but for the warrior caste their Sun-god was *Indra*, whilst for the priestly caste the Sun-god was *Surya*.

Nuada Argetlam, the primitive Irish Sun-god.

Nudd (or *Ludd*), was an ancient British Sun-god, the equivalent of the Irish *Nuada Argetlam*.

Osiris, the great Egyptian divinity. Began as a local god of Busiris, and regarded as a great benefactor of Egypt. He later became a Sun-god and a Moon-god, through being identified with *Ra* and *Khuns*.

Pushan, a Vedic Sun-god.

Quetzalcoatl, Aztec virgin-born Sun-god and saviour, eventually displaced by *Tezcatlipoca* who was probably also worshipped by the Mayas.

Ra, ancient Egyptian Sun-god.

Savitri (or *Savitar*), an all-powerful Hindu Sun-god identified with the Surya.

Shamash (or *Shemesh*, *Samas*), Babylonian Sun-god. Worshipped also by the Assyrians. At a later date displaced by *Marduk*, which had previously been the name of the Jupiter deity.

Sol, the early Roman Sun-god.

Soranus, a Sabine divinity, usually identified with Apollo.

Surya, Indian Sun-god, who was known as the Eye of the Gods. One of five solar deities. Is the Hindu equivalent of the Greek *Helios*.

Tammuz, early Sun-god of the Canaanites (see Ezekiel 8:14).

Tezcatlipoca, one of the chief gods of the ancient Mexicans. Was first a sky-god and later a Sun-god.

Thorr, Nordic Sun-god, also a storm-god, and possibly meant to be the Scandinavian *Thor* identified with Jupiter.

Usil, the Sun; corresponding to Apollo (the *Aplu* of the Etruscans); an object of worship rather than a god.

Uz, the Akkadian Goat-god, was a solar deity who, clad in goat skins, presided over the revolution of the Sun.

Vishnu, an Indian deity who is a Sun-god in one of his manifestations.

Zoroaster, mighty Sun-god of ancient Persia, and said to be the inventor of magic.

Finally, we may still see today how the worship of the Sun is symbolized in the Japanese national flag, a rising Sun.

The Moon

The Moon has been worshipped both as god and goddess. Essentially, as a goddess, she has represented fertility, the Great Mother, Mother Earth and the fruits of the Earth.

Aah, an Egyptian Moon-god.

Alilat, an Arabian Moon and fertility goddess. Also called *Ilat*.

Amar-Tudda, the Moon-god, the "Lusty-bull", of the Akkadians.

Artemis, called *Diana* by the Romans, one of the great divinities of the Greeks. Was the Greek Moon-goddess before *Selene*. Sister of Apollo, the Sun-god.

Asherah, a Canaanite Moon and fertility goddess.

Ashtoreth, Phoenician and Zidonian Moon-goddess. Ashtoreth is possibly a lengthening of the name of the Assyrio-Babylonian goddess *Istar*. Ashtoreth and Istar are sometimes identified with the planet Venus. Worshipped by Solomon (I Kings 11:5 and II Kings 23:13). Identified with the Roman and Greek goddess *Astarte*.

Astarte, Grecian Moon-goddess. *Astarta* means "queen of heaven".

Ataensic, American Indians' Moon-goddess.

Axiokerse, Samothrakian Moon-goddess.

Bendis, the Thracian Moon-goddess.

Britomartis, a Creton nymph, daughter of Zeus and beloved by Minos, who pursued her for nine months, till at length she leapt into the sea and was changed by Artemis into a goddess. Assumed to be a Moon-goddess.

Cybele, ancient Moon-goddess. "The Great Mother". Identical with *Ceres*, the ancient Roman goddess, *Ops*, an ancient Roman fertility goddess, *Rhaa*, an ancient earth-goddess, and *Vesta*.

Demeter, one of the great divinities of the Greeks, was regarded as the protectoress of agriculture and of all the fruits of the Earth. Called *Ceres* by the Romans.

Diana, an ancient Italian divinity, whom the Romans identified with the Greek *Artemis*. As Dianus, or the god of light, represented by the Sun, so Diana, the goddess of light, was represented by the Moon. Diana was also the name given to the Moon-god of the Ephesians.

En-Zu, the early Sumerians' Moon-god, which means the lord of knowledge, because it was through him that they learned to regulate the year and also the festival of the gods.

Freyr, Moon-god and chief god of fertility in Norway and Sweden.

Hecate, a mysterious Greek divinity, a Moon-goddess, and also thought to be an earth-goddess. She was honoured by all the immortal gods, and the extensive power possessed by her was probably the reason that she was subsequently identified with several other divinities. Hence she is said to have been *Selene* or *Luna* in heaven, *Artemis* or *Diana* in earth, and *Persephone* or *Proserpina* in the lower world.

Hurakan, early Nordic Moon-god and storm-god.

Io, name of a deified priestess of Hera, representing the Moon and the female principle in creation. Thought to be the same as *Isis*.

Isis, one of the chief Egyptian divinities, wife of Osiris and mother of Horus. She was originally the Earth-goddess, and afterwards the Moon-goddess. The Greeks identified her both with *Demeter* and with *Io*.

Istar (or *Ishtar*), the Sumero-Akkadian Moon-goddess. Was afterwards especially connected with the planet Venus, but was always chiefly lunar in Syria and Phoenicia.

Itzamna, Mayan Moon-god and one of the most important of their deities.

Juno, a Moon-goddess and earth-goddess, and "Queen of the Heavens". Identical with *Hera*.

Khonsu, Egyptian Moon-god.

Lamga, Euphratian Moon-god.

Lebhana-Leukothea, Persian Moon-goddess.

Losna, the Moon, equivalent to the Roman *Diana*, an object of worship by the Etruscans, rather than a god.

Lucina, ancient Roman Moon-goddess, who presided over pregnant women.

Luna, Greek goddess of the Moon, identified with *Selene*.

Mani, ancient Scandinavian Moon-goddess.

Mēn, Moon-god of the Phrygians of Asia Minor.

Meni, probable Moon-god of Canaanitish nations.

Metztli, Aztec Moon-goddess.

Nanna, Nordic Moon-god.

Nannar, primary name of the Euphratean Moon-god, written *Na-an-nar*. He is styled the Strong Bull whose horn is powerful. From a Euphratean centre the idea and the cult of a lunar god or goddess connected with the bull, ox and cow, spread alike to India and to the far West.

Parvati, the Moon-goddess of the Hindus. A personification of *Sakti*, thus representing the principle of fertility and the Great Mother. Sometimes referred to as *Durga*.

Selene, the Greek Moon-goddess, identified in later times with *Artemis*. In classical times she is styled *Taurokerôs*, and her statue at Elis had horns from the head.

Shing-Moo, Chinese Moon-goddess, "Queen of the Heavens".

Sin, Euphratean Moon-god, at times described as the sire of *Samas*, the Sun-god, night preceding day. Considered superior to Samas.

Soma, Hindu Moon-god.

Subhadra, Hindu Moon-god, "the glorious mover in the circle".

Susa-No-O, Japanese Moon-god.

Thoth, Egyptian Moon-god of learning and wisdom, an inventor of magic.

Ur, Oriental Moon-god, or god of light. Also an Assyrian fire-god.

Mercury

Essentially, the deities associated with Mercury were of a versatile nature, and were believed to possess the attributes of a divine messenger, scribe, and inventor of commerce, science and education.

Anbai, the name given to the divinity of the planet Mercury by the South Arabians. Identified with *Nabiu*, the prophet and messenger of the gods. Thus, Anbai or the Star of Nabiu was identified with Hermes and became the Star of Hermes or the Latin Mercurius.

Hermes, the divine winged Grecian god. In Greek mythology Zeus made Hermes "messenger or herald of the gods". He was the god of eloquence, of public speaking, of prudence and cunning, both in words and actions. He was endowed with shrewdness and sagacity, and was regarded as the author of many inventions, including the alphabet, the lyre, music, astronomy, numbers, gymnastics, and weights and measures. He was also the god of roads, guiding travellers; and the god of commerce.

Mercury or *Mercurius*, the important Roman divinity of commerce and merchandise and gain, patron of wisdom and learning, the guide who directed the souls of the dead to the

Other World. Identified with the Greek Hermes. The
Romans eventually transferred all the attributes and myths
of Hermes to their own god.

Nabiu or *Nabu*, the god of science and learning among the
Babylonians and Assyrians. He was the scribe of the gods,
lord of books and writing.

Nebo (Babylonian *Nabium*), may be identical with *Nabiu* or
Nabu. Was the scribe of the gods, and supposed to be the
inventor of writing, and the deity who presided over science
and learning. The titles of "scribe of the universe", "admini-
strator of the hosts of heaven and earth", are applied to him
in the cuneiform inscriptions.

Turms, Etruscan deity, corresponding to *Hermes* and *Mercury*.

Woden, the most widely honoured of the heathen gods in
ancient England. Identified with the Roman *Mercury* and
the same god as the Germanic *Wodan*. A primitive West
European god (*Wodenaz, Wuotan*, and in Old Norse, *Voden*
and later *Odinn*). The Romans called the fourth day of the
week *Mercurii dies*, after Mercury, and when the Britains
under the Roman influence adopted the calendar of Rome
they called this same day *Wodnes-daeg*, after their god
Woden. Later, of course, this came to be called Wednesday.
Woden was the god of wisdom, trade, and negotiating.

Venus

The deities identified with Venus were goddesses of love,
beauty, promiscuity, fertility.

Aphrodite, the Grecian goddess of love, licentiousness and
beauty, to whom prostitutes were dedicated. Identified with the
Roman goddess *Venus*. Among her many loves was her love
for Ares the god of War. Aphrodite derives from *fero*, to bear,
bring forth, or produce. She was the mother of Eros (Cupid).

Cypris or *Kypris*, the patron goddess of Cyprus.

Freyja, powerful Scandinavian fertility goddess, sister of Freyr
(Moon-god). Goddess of a cult especially concerned with
marriage rites, erotic love, helping women in childbirth. The
two-fold aspect of all fertility goddesses appears to be that as
mother and lover.

Frig or *Frigg*, Old English goddess of fertility identified with Roman *Venus*. Connected with an Indo-European root, *Prij*, meaning "love". In her earlier Germanic form, *Frija*, she gave her name to the sixth day of the week, Friday. She was the wife of Wodan (Mars). A Mother Goddess.

Great Mother Cybele, the name under which Venus was worshipped in Asia Minor.

Istar, the Sumero-Akkadian goddess, variously named. She is the Semitic *Ashtoreth*. The Grecian *Astarte*, originally representing the Moon in its female phase, *Ashtoreth Qarnaim*, but Istar was subsequently identified with the planet Venus. The planetary Istar is double-phased as the Morning-star, goddess of War, and the Evening-star, goddess of Love. The planet Venus was called by the Greeks, *Hesper-Phospher*, which came to be known as the Star of Aphrodite. Also identified with *Ishtar* by the Euphrateans, corresponding to the goddess of love and beauty of the Greeks of a later period (Venus). Another name for Istar as the planet Venus was *Ninsianna* ("Lady-of-the-garden-of-heaven").

Lucifer or *Phosphorus*, that is, the bringer of light, is the Grecian name for the planet Venus when seen in the morning before sunrise. Was also called *Hesperus, Vesperugo, Vesper, Noctifer,* or *Nocturnus,* when it appeared after sunset.

Turan, Etruscan deity corresponding to Aphrodite and Venus.

Venus, originally a Latin goddess of the spring. One of the earliest of Roman goddesses, whose attributes and worship were extended after her identification with the Greek Aphrodite. She was the goddess of love, of sensual pleasure, of beauty, and of fertility.

Mars

The deities identified with Mars were representatives of war, carnage, death, storm, plague, or were the slayers of dragons.

Ares, the Greek god of war, one of the great Olympian gods. Identified with the Roman *Mars*.

Attis-Adonis, the name by which Mars was worshipped in Asia-Minor.

Belatucadrus, a god worshipped in Roman Britain. Altars to this deity have been found in England, and in some altars he is identified with the Roman deity, Mars.

Cocideus (or *Cocidus*), in Roman Britain altars in Cumberland were dedicated to this god, identified with the Roman deity, Mars.

Hercules, said to be the personification of Mars, not of the Sun. In *The Text-Book of Astrology*, Alfred J. Pearce writes, "Hyginus says, 'The third planet is Mars, which others called Hercules.' Macrobius says, 'Maro with the ripeness of profound learning, refers the Salii to Hercules, because the priests consider that god the same as Mars.' The same is affirmed in the 'Menippea' of Varo, entitled 'The other Hercules,' in which, after much discourse about Hercules, this god was proved to be Mars. The star which all others call Mars, is called Hercules by the Chaldeans."

Indra, said by some authorities to be the Hindu equivalent of Mars, as a slayer of serpents and dragons, though it seems more likely that this deity, as a storm-god, was most correctly identified with Jupiter.

Mamers, the Oscan name of the god associated with Mars.

Mars, an ancient Roman god, identified with the Greek *Ares*. He was the god of war, and war itself was frequently designated by the name of Mars. He was originally the Romans' nature-god, the guardian of crops and herds, warding off pests, storms and droughts.

Nergal (or *Nirgal*), the Euphratean god of war and hunting, for whom Mars was said to be the star of. Identified with the Roman Mars.

Odin, the mighty Northern European god of battle, of death, and of inspiration and victory. Rites said to belong to Odin are piercing by a spear, hanging, and burning. Some ancient tribes practised terrible rites, to appease the lord of war by the shedding of blood. Identified later with the Roman Mars.

Tiwaz, Germanic god of battle identified with the Roman Mars.

Tyr, an early Scandinavian war-god identified with Mars.

Wodan (or *Wotan*), war-god worshipped by the heathen Germanic peoples and associated with the Roman Mars. Said to be succeeded by Odin.

Zalbat, Euphratean war-god.

Jupiter

The deities identified with Jupiter were variously known as gods of thunder and storms, learning, wisdom, justice, seership.

Bussumarus, a Celtic god, later identified by the Romans with their Jupiter.

Donar, thunder-god of the heathen Germans, predecessor of Thor. The day sacred to Jupiter, Thursday, was dedicated to the German thunder-god, *Donnerstag*.

Indra, the Hindu thunder-god as well as sun-god. Attributed with many of Thor's characteristics and considered to be Thor's counterpart.

Jupiter, the mighty Roman deity, the most powerful and the highest among the gods. Originally an elemental divinity, his name signifying the father or lord of heaven. Thus he was worshipped as the god of storms, thunder, lightning and rain. The Romans believed that he determined the source of all human affairs. He presided over the great Roman games. He was the seer who foresaw the future, and was the god invoked at the beginning of every undertaking. He was the guardian of law, protector of justice and virtue. As the lord of heaven and the prince of light, the white colour was sacred to him, and white animals were sacrificed to him. Identified with Zeus of the Greeks.

Marduk (*Merodach* of the Bible), Babylonian (Euphratean) god which the planet Jupiter was said to be an aspect of. Robert Eisler in *The Royal Art of Astrology* says that the god was "a personification of the spring sun drying the soil after the inundations, restoring order from chaos, the slayer of the dragon, the builder of the celestial house and organiser of the world. He produces storms as his weapons in the fight against the primeval monster." At a later period the name Marduk came to be applied to the Sun.

Thor, the mighty Scandinavian thunder-god, whose cult had a long life in Western Europe. His symbol was a hammer. In his association with the natural world he was both destroyer and protector. His equation with the Roman Hercules suggests that many of his attributes were akin to those of the personification of Mars. He was called upon to hallow and protect the many aspects of men's lives in the community. Identified with the Roman Jupiter and the Greek Zeus.

Thunor, old Anglo-Saxon thunder-god identified with the Roman Jupiter. He was the protector of the world against giants, and had power over the weather, especially storms. When the Roman calendar was accepted in Britain after A.D. 300 the Britains named the fifth day of the week *Thunresdaeg* (Thursday).

Tinia, the chief Etruscan god, corresponding to the Greek Zeus and the Roman Jupiter.

Zeus, the greatest of the Olympian gods, identified with Jupiter by the Romans. Zeus presided over the heavens and the upper regions of the world. He is called the father of gods and of men, the most high and powerful among the immortals, whom all other deities obey. The supreme ruler who manages everything; the founder of law and order. Even fate itself was subordinate to him. He is armed with thunder and lightning. Jupiter was clearly the "star of Zeus".

Saturn

The deities identified with Saturn were essentially gods of death, time-cycles, reaping, darkness, strife, agriculture, social order.

Chiun (or *Kewan*, *Kaimanu*), Babylonian name for Saturn as a god, and thought to be worshipped as a god by the Israelites (Amos 5:26). It may be noteworthy that Saturn gives its name to the seventh day of our week, "Saturn's day" (Saturday), the sabbath of the Jewish week.

Cronus (or *Chronos*, *Kronos*), the Greek god of time and of mundane time-cycles, who was originally a harvest-god. Said to be identified with Chiun of the Babylonians.

Kakkab Pes (star of the Boar), another Euphratean name for Saturn. One of the two principle divinities of the Euphratean pantheon was *Ninip-Ber*. *Ber* is the "Lord-of-the-Boar", and a god of the planet Saturn. This animal has been referred to in myth as "the Boar of the storm and darkness".

Ninib (or *Ninip*), Euphratean god of strife, specially connected with Kronos and Saturn.

Ninurta, Babylonian god of death, associated with Saturn.

Saturnus, a mythical king of Italy, whom the Romans identified with the Greek Cronos. The planet Saturn was personified by the Romans as Saturnus, god of agriculture, and the reputed founder of civilization and social order. The name, *Saturnus*, was said to have derived from sowing (*sero, sevi, satum*). His reign was presumably the golden age of Italy.

Uranus

This planet was unknown to the ancients, being discovered in 1781. It was first named Herschel, after its discoverer, Sir William Herschel. But before it was given this name, others had proposed that the new planet be called Uranus. According to Camille Flammarion in his *Popular Astronomy* the reason for Uranus being suggested was that this was the name of the most ancient deity of all, the father of Saturn, "to whom reparation was due for so many centuries of neglect". But for a long time the planet bore the name of Herschel. However, to quote Flammarion, "custom has since declared for the mythological appellation, and Jupiter, Saturn, and Uranus succeed each other in order of descent—son, father, and grandfather". In mythology Uranus or Heaven was the Greek name for the personification of the night sky. Uranus was sometimes called a son and sometimes the husband of *Gaea* or *Ge* (Earth). This is because Ge as the personification of the Earth is described as the first being that sprang from Chaos, and gave birth to Uranus (Heaven) and Pontus (Sea). By Uranus she became the mother of the Titans (six sons and six daughters) who were hated by their father. Ge therefore concealed them in the bosom of the Earth. She made a large iron sickle with which Cronos, one of the sons, cut off his father's genitals.

There is undoubtedly a reason for this planet being named Uranus, and to what extent the human psychological traits associated with this factor in a birth-chart can be connected with the myths surrounding this deity of the same name still needs to be clarified by scholars qualified for this study. Uranus (the planet and its correlated drives in human psychology as symbolized in a birth-chart) represent an archetype of the collective unconscious. I can always feel inspired to further my own understanding of myths when I think of a passage written by Hilda Davidson in her *Gods and Myths of Northern Europe*.[4] She writes that in our study of myths we can see these "as man's attempt to embody his intuitive ideas about the human mind and its environment, to express truths dimly perceived which have roots in his innermost being. Thus the myths may lead us to discover more about our spiritual heritage, and perhaps to realize some of the defects in the spiritual development of the modern world. The study of mythology need no longer be looked on as an escape from reality into the fantasies of primitive peoples, but as a search for the deeper understanding of the human mind. In reaching out to explore the distant hills where the gods dwell and the deeps where the monsters are lurking, we are perhaps discovering the way home."

Neptune

This planet was first recognized through a telescope in September 1846, in the exact location calculated by a young French mathematician, Urbain Leverrier. And yet a year before a Cambridge student, John Couch Adams, had carried out the same computations as a result of the deviation of Uranus from its calculated orbit. His professor, however, who had assigned him the task, had not bothered to look for the predicted planet through the excellent telescope at Cambridge Observatory. This planet was discovered, not by chance, "but by the visionary powers of pure intellect, by computation from the universal law of gravitation".[5] Why was this planet named *Neptune*? According to Camille Flammarion, there were some who wished to call the planet by the name "of the learned mathematician who had discovered it 'at the end of his pen'; but mythological memories prevailed again, as they had done for the Herschel planet, and the name of Neptune, son of Saturn, god of the sea, already proposed for Uranus, was given by common consent to the star of Leverrier".[6] And so there are those among us who would say that, just as the prediction and discovery of the physical planet called Neptune was not by chance, neither was it chance that gave the planet this name. I, for one, believe that at that time an archetypal force from within the collective unconscious influenced the choice of name. I can think of no other explanation, when in my own experience the life-principle attributed to this Neptunian archetype is found to correlate so accurately with psychological traits and environmental conditions that can be predicted from the placing of Neptune in an individual birth-chart. Possibly a wealth of fresh information concerning this Neptunian archetype may be uncovered by scholars who could delve deeply into its mythological associations. However, the following deities would seem to have a common connection with Neptune.

Aegir, Norse sea-god compared with the Greek Poseidon.

Consus, an ancient Roman divinity who was identified in later times with Neptune. Hence Livy calls him Neptunus Equestris. He was regarded by some as the god of secret deliberations, but he was most probably a god of the lower world.

Neptunus, the chief marine divinity of the Romans, but as the early Romans were not a maritime people scarcely anything is known of the worship of the Italian god of this name. Roman poets completely identified Neptune with the Greek Poseidon, and accordingly all the attributes of the latter have been bestowed on Neptunus (or Neptune).

Nethuns, Etruscan god of water, corresponding closely to Neptune the Roman sea-god.

Poseidon, the Greek sea-god, identified with Neptunus by the Romans. In the Homeric poems he is described as equal to Zeus in dignity, but less powerful. He is said to have created the horse. The symbol of Poseidon's power was the trident, with which he used to shatter rocks, to call forth or subdue storms, to shake the earth.

Varuna, the marine deity of the Hindus.

Pluto

The prediction of a trans-Neptunian planet was made years before its eventual discovery on 21 January 1930 at the Lowell Observatory at Flagstaff, Arizona, U.S.A. As early as 1915

Percival Lowell and other astronomers had begun calculating the possible position of this hypothetical planet. How did this planet receive the name Pluto? In the magazine *Zenit*, 1931, on page 202 appeared the following: "As reported in *Science*, Vol. 7, No. 1850, 1930, Pluto had been called simply *Planet X* at the time of its discovery. After publication of the discovery of the planet a little English girl, eleven-year-old Venetia Burney, of Oxford, submitted the first proposal for the name Pluto. Her father telegraphed this name at once to the Lowell Observatory, and as this was the first proposal to arrive in Flagstaff, it was accepted."

One might well be excused for showing complete surprise that upon the suggested name for this planet by a little girl, astrologers have seemingly based all their theories, many of which are traceable to attributes of Hades and Pluto, gods of the underworld in mythology. It would, of course, be incorrect to say that *all* theories are a result of the name Pluto's mythological connections, as serious astrologers also produce theories based on personal experience and investigation of large numbers of birth-charts.

Pluto or *Pluton* was the name given to an ancient pagan Sun-god, but he was best known in Greek mythology as the giver of wealth. *Dis* was the name under which the Gauls worshipped Pluto, god of Hell. It was also the name the Romans sometimes gave to Pluto, and hence also to the lower world. *Hades* (originally *Aides*), was the god of the nether or lower world. In ordinary life he was usually called Pluto because people did not like to pronounce the dreaded name of Hades. Hades was son of Cronus and Rhea, and brother of Zeus and Poseidon, and with his wife, Persephone, he ruled over the souls of the dead. To quote from *A Smaller Classical Dictionary*,[7] "In the division of the world among the 3 brothers, Hades obtained the nether world, the abode of the shades, over which he ruled. His character is described as fierce and inexorable, whence of all the gods he was most hated by mortals. The sacrifices offered to him and Persephone consisted of black sheep; and the person who offered the sacrifice had to turn away his face. The ensign of his power was a staff, with which, like Hermes, he drove the shades into the lower world. . . . He possessed a helmet which rendered the wearer invisible, and which he sometimes lent to both gods and men. . . . Being the king of the lower world, Pluto is the giver of all the blessings that come from the earth: hence he gives the metals contained in the earth, and is called Pluto." An Etruscan god of the underworld, identified with the Roman Pluto and with Hades, was called *Mantus*.

NOTES

1. *Before Philosophy*, by H. and H. A. Frankfort, p. 12 (Penguin Books).
2. *Primitive Constellations*, Vol. 2, by Robert Brown, p. 224 (William & Norgate).
3. *Ibid.*, pp. 224–5.
4. P. 22 (Penguin Books, 1964).
5. *And There Was Light*, by Rudolf Thiel, p. 273 (Mentor Books, The New American Library).
6. *Popular Astronomy*, by Camille Flammarion, p. 467 (Chatto & Windus, London, 1907).
7. (Publishers: J. M. Dent & Sons, Ltd.).

5 Self-Integration; Actuation

Archetypal Processes

The Sun, Moon and planets each symbolize archetypal processes within the collective unconscious. These are seen as *basic patterns of emotional and mental behaviour* in man, because the archetype represents or personifies certain instinctive data of the primitive psyche, and indicates the existence of definite forms in the psychic system which are present always and everywhere and are universal and identical in all individuals. In Chapter 10 a fuller explanation is given of the archetype.

Because each planet symbolizes an archetype this does not mean that no other archetypal processes are associated with the planet's function within the psyche. As Jung has said, there are as many archetypes as there are typical situations in life. It may be that the very name "archetype" conjures up in the mind of some readers a sort of mystical god-figure. This is not so. We might reasonably say that the archetypes represent patterns of *instinctual* behaviour. Like the morphological elements of the human body the archetypes are *inherited* structural elements of the human psyche which antedate all conscious experience. The archetype is essentially an unconscious content, and it is when a situation occurs which corresponds to a given archetype, that archetype becomes activated and a *compulsiveness* appears and the individual reacts to the situation accordingly, though in his own individual manner. We each contain within ourselves the primary function or archetypal content or process with which we associate the Sun astrologically: the desire to achieve wholeness of being, the need for self-integration. But in reacting to this unconsciously originating compulsiveness, or deep-rooted drive for wholeness of being, we will inevitably encounter situations and external forces and stimuli which will activate other archetypal contents with which we can associate the Sun: the need to be creative, to organize, to lead others, to be self-sufficient and so on.

In Chapters 5 to 8 the archetypal processes correlated with the Sun, Moon and planets will be interpreted in psychological terms. Even if a reader finds it difficult to think in terms of Jungian concepts (the archetype, anima, the self, persona, etc.) most of the psychological indications given should be easily understood. Examples will be given as a guide to the interpreting of planets within the framework of an individual chart, using the chart reproduced on this page.

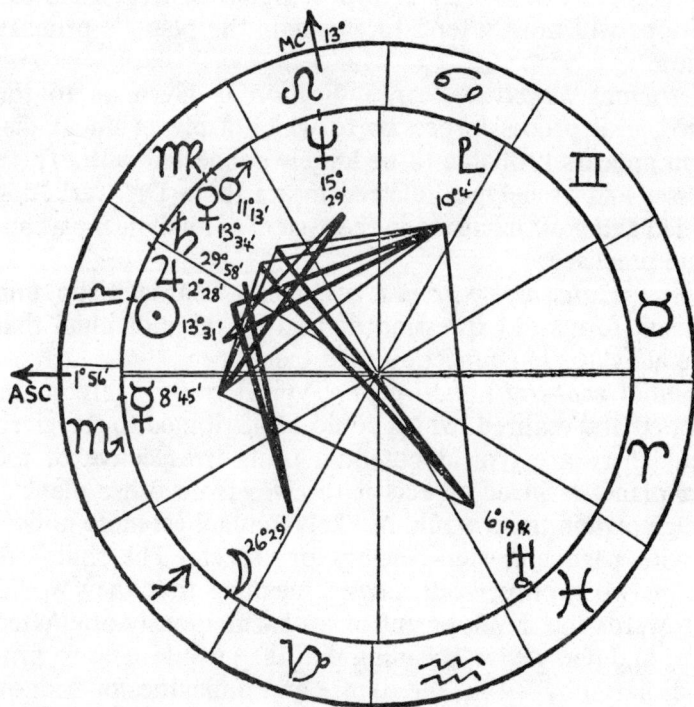

Fig. 1.   Birth-chart of a male subject.

Each archetypal process or psychological function symbolized by a planet is interpreted under certain headings, and a few words of explanation might be helpful at this point.

Primary function. This implies the process within the psyche which a planet seems likely to be most significantly associated with.

Definition. A concise explanation of what is meant by the primary function, so that the symbolism of the planet can be clearly understood for the purpose of practical chart interpretation.

Further definitions. Various forms of interpreting psychological processes connected with the planet. Readers will recognize numerous traditional correlations, and the author has made a number of suggestions based on his own experience of the planetary functions. It will be noted that these further definitions will mostly tend to elucidate the planet's primary function.

Contributes largely to. An indication is given as to the psychological process/processes to which a planet under discussion appears probable to be largely connected with. These processes and archetypes referred to are those Dr. Carl Jung classified and gave names to in the system of analytical psychology he practised.

Characteristic desire trends activated. Characteristic and significant forms of expression desired by the individual that can be activated in connection with the planet.

Potential root-traits motivated. Typical traits likely to be motivated and realized, which could be attributed to the given planet. These are typical potential traits irrespective of the sign a planet is in or aspects it receives from other planets, although certain traits would be likely to manifest more noticeably with particular sign-placings or aspects. The traits are listed in two groups: *constructive,* meaning that they would help towards the development of an harmoniously-orientated nature; and *destructive,* meaning that they would tend to produce disharmony within the nature and difficulties or friction between the subject and his environment.

Traditional association with. A variety of matters are listed which traditionally have been associated with a given planet. These can give the reader a further insight to the primary function within man which a given planet is associated with.

Practical interpretation. An explanation of how one might

attempt to interpret the Sun or Moon or planet from one's own birth-chart, in practical and commonsense terms. Only very brief guidance can be given in relation to the signs, houses and aspects, as entire books are needed to cover these features thoroughly. These books will in due course be included in *The Astrologer's Handbook Series*. Reference is made to the example chart reproduced on page 65.

Interaction with Environment

Man is born as a result of environmental forces and activities, and he spends his entire life learning to successfully and harmoniously interact with his environment. Each employs his own unique and yet inevitably linked system of mental, nervous and sensory organs for the development of his consciousness and skills, that he may survive the stresses and pressures and dangerous situations which interaction with the environment brings.

But man's life is not simply a matter of the individual organism resisting, avoiding and combating the forces of the external world. The environment influences a man's development in many ways. The growth processes are necessarily dependent on environment. A man's habits and skills depend upon environmental situations enabling practice, and thus the environment provides opportunity and stimulation. The organism appropriates and uses things from the environment. A man's knowledge depends on the teaching he has received from his environment, and his social attitudes depend on the social situations in which he has participated and enabled him to develop and express his type and mode of potentialities.

A man's birth-chart is indeed a unique system of revealing his potential abilities for adapting himself to his environment, and of indicating the most natural modes of reaction he might successfully apply to environmental stimulation and challenge. In Chapters 5 to 8 the Sun, Moon and each planet is necessarily treated as if it were a separate function within the psychic structure of man. The cosmic bodies are shown to symbolize the vital processes man inherits as archetypal contents of his unconscious being, from which he learns to develop his modes of interaction with his environment . . . self-integration, actuation, communication, co-ordination, evaluation, self-projection, self-expansion, self-control, deviation, refinement, transformation. But the reader must realize that no function can be correctly interpreted as an isolated feature of the psyche. It is through the overall pattern of the birth-chart that we can learn to understand the interdependence of each function so that the structure of the individual psyche can be interpreted as a whole, and the individual's potential and unique form of achieving a successful interaction with his environment can be clearly judged.

The Sun (☉)

Primary function: Self-integration.

Definition: To achieve wholeness and uniqueness of being through the integration of the varied components of the psyche, and so that each component functions to its fullest potential as an integral part of the whole.

Further definitions:

(a) *Self-realization.* The fulfilment by one's own efforts of the possibilities of development of potentialities, and the acceptance of one's limitations.

(b) *Self-sufficiency.* The need to feel adequately qualified and competent to cope with inner psychic forces and with the demands of the environment. The need to be *self-confident*.

(c) The need to have the ability to *synthesize*, to integrate and organize the varied and contrasting features of one's make-up into a complex whole, and not have them as disintegrated and unbalanced parts. The need to have the ability to synthesize the entire range of one's interests and activities, and to be in authority, powerful and influential.

(d) The *masculine principle*. The need to assert authority, strength, will-power, and command respect. The need to be fully conscious of one's actions, as symbolized by the *Logos* and the *archetypal father*: "The father is the representative of the spirit, whose function it is to oppose pure instinctuality."[1] "Gaining consciousness, formulating ideas— that is the father-principle of the Logos, which in endless struggles extricates itself ever and again from the mother's womb, from the realm of the unconscious."[2]

Contributes largely to:

(a) The unfoldment of the *self* and the development of the *ego*. Jung has called the self the central archetype, the archetype of order, the principle and archetype of orientation and meaning. "The self is not only the centre but also the whole circumference which embraces both consciousness and unconscious; it is the centre of this totality, just as the ego is the centre of the conscious mind."[3] The ego is that part of the conscious mind with which we normally identify ourselves, and it is the only content of the self that we do know. Jung has said that the self "is our life's goal, for it is the completest expression of that fateful combination we call individuality".[4]

(b) The *superior function*, which determines the individual's type. There are four functions which we use to orientate ourselves in the world: sensation, thinking, feeling, and intuition. Every individual adapts himself to reality most easily and most successfully by means of one function, which is called the superior function, and which gives the conscious attitude its direction and quality.

(c) The process of *individuation*, and the *reconciliation of the opposing trends of one's nature*. "Individuation means becoming an 'in-dividual', and, in so far as 'individuality' embraces our innermost, last, and incomparable uniqueness, it also implies becoming one's own self. We could therefore translate individuation as 'coming to selfhood' or 'self-realization'."[5]

Characteristic desire trends activated: Ambition, urge for power, leadership, creativeness, constructiveness, self-reliance, organization and administration, masculinity, individuality.

Potential root-traits motivated:

1. *Constructive*
   Generosity, dignity, pride, self-assurance, independence, loyalty, gallantry, strength of will, purposefulness, dependableness, creativeness, conscientiousness, executive ability.

2. *Destructive*
   Self-centredness, egotism, incompetence, ostentation, pompousness, boastfulness, destructiveness, aggressiveness or timidity, dominance.

Traditional association with: Generating power, procreation, bringing into being, the monarchy or other supreme authority in the State, positions of rank or title, Government or public officials, celebrities, the father, judges, superiors generally, powerful or influential friends, the source of "heart-felt" desires.

Practical interpretation

The actual interpretation of each chart factor will not be given, as such detailed work would need the space of an entire book to give it justice. As has already been mentioned, books on actual interpretation will appear in *The Astrologer's Handbook Series*. At present, you will be given indications, for instance, of how to prepare your interpretation of the Sun.

The function in man symbolized by the Sun is the self-generating force for regulating and maintaining equilibrium between all components of the human organism or psyche. What would appear to be the other most important psychic components are those symbolized by the Moon and the planets and the angles of the chart. Thus, a birth-chart for a given moment is a blue-print of a unique arrangement of an individual psyche, from which can be interpreted the special relationship between the components in terms of:

(*a*) potentially dominant attitudes or drives;
(*b*) potentially inhibiting or limited (in manifestation) attitudes or drives;
(*c*) sources of potential conflict (disharmony, lack of cohesion) and greatest tension and stress.

How do we begin to assess a chart-pattern and hence to understand the potential stresses and dominant features which compose an individual psyche? There is no cut-and-dried formula, but for convenience there is no better starting-point than the Sun.

We must always think of the Sun as the *centre of gravity* of the individual, and as such the Sun must be the central reference point to which we relate each factor in the chart as well as the pattern of the chart as a whole.

Let us turn to the example chart on page 65. The primary function of the Sun is *self-integration*. How might this particular subject whose chart we are looking at try to achieve this ideal, self-integration, a balanced, perfectly fulfilled state of being, the goal of individuation? That is too much to expect any astrologer or psycho-analyst to define with complete accuracy. But we *can*, with care, indicate significant clues as to the *nature* of the individual psyche and its potentially strongest and also weakest features, hence its probable sources of most easily produced stresses and disharmony, the knowledge of which could help the individual to achieve some greater measure of self-realization.

A very, very important point which I am always instructing my students to remember when interpreting a birth-chart, is that the chart-pattern can only indicate the *potentialities* of the person in question. To what degree each factor in the chart will manifest as recognizable behaviour or as a definite attitude will depend upon the person's childhood upbringing, education, the constantly changing environmental conditions, and, most important, their own personal values and choice of positive or negative reactions to situations. But the blue-print of potentialities and of the limiting psychic structure is ever there within them, and to accurately describe this blue-print is the greatest benefit of astrology.

If the Sun represents the subject's need for self-integration, we first look at the example chart to find where this central reference point is situated—its psychic orientation to the other components of the chart. It is in Libra (♎) in the 12th house. This tells us that a very important attitude and mode of response by the subject to his environment, and which *should* be a mode most naturally developed, will be comprised of typical Libran traits. Whether by archetypal compulsion in the form of unconscious motivation, or through conscious thought and effort (especially connected with the *ego*), the subject should tend to react to situations and *try to organize* his own complex range of potentialities in a manner typical of Libra.

But the Libran traits will not necessarily be expressed true to type, as these will tend to be modified by Venus (ruler of the Sun-sign, Libra) being in Virgo(♍) and ♂♂, ♂♅. Other significant behaviour-patterns and likely sources of tension and stress, or sources of dynamic psychic responses, vital to the process of self-realization and for the development of new forms of conscious awareness (to the self and to his environ-ment) can be gleaned from ☉⚹MC/♆, □♇. The 12th house placing of the Sun could introduce difficulties as this area of the chart can prove self-inhibiting, and yet it also can have an advantage in correlating with an innate suitability for self-expression through work and interests where the need for limelight and self-exposure is preferably not sought after.

No interpretation of the function associated with the Sun would be complete without, of course, relating all other com-ponents of the chart to this centre of gravity. This procedure enables one to assess where integration is especially needed in the areas of the psyche most vulnerable to stress (e.g. the com-bined affect of two planets forming a difficult aspect); and types of behaviour one is less likely to adopt because it may be that their motivating responses are mostly unconscious and not readily awakened, suggested by signs not containing planets or an angle (such as ♑ ♈ ♊ in our example chart). Of probable next importance to the Sun as a dominant feature that also contributes to the composition of the *superior function* is the *Ascendant* or Rising Sign that is evaluated together with the planet/planets ruling that sign. But this must be the subject of another book.

The Moon (☽)

Primary function: Actuation.

Definition: The *actuating* of life-processes: the function neces-sary for bringing a process into action, for animating psychic processes with active properties.

Further definitions:

(a) The Sun is the source of all life-energy, but without the function symbolized by the Moon man would be denied

SELF-INTEGRATION; ACTUATION   73

vital animation and expression of physical, mental and emotional *activity*. In myths the Sun and Moon have been portrayed as the parents of life, male and female respectively. Astrologically, too, the Sun and Moon have been associated with the masculine and feminine principles. But contrary to accepted opinion I would say that this is not strictly true in every expression of the Moon's function. Essentially the Moon's function is a feminine role as can be seen in its apparent connection with the *anima* in man and the *persona* of a woman; yet this function also works through the masculine *persona* in a man and the masculine *animus* in a woman. The essence of its function is, it would seem, the actuating of life-processes. Just as the male sperm would be uncreative without its union with the female ovum, so we will find in psychological terms that the traits associated with the Sun must have the Moon function's actuating co-operation for the psyche as a whole to fulfil itself as an *active* organism.

(*b*) The *feminine principle*. The need to nurture and protect others; receptiveness, impressionability, the powerful emotional content, sensitivity, moodiness: traits that are clearly evident where the Moon is a dominant factor in an individual's birth-chart.

(*c*) A necessary *rhythmic ebb and flow of energy* as the function mediates between the *ego* and the outside world and between the ego and the inner world. Reflected frequently in alternating moods, fluctuations in temperament, restlessness.

(*d*) The function that is necessarily *sensitive to environment*, as a (largely inherited) system of psychic adaptation, and for the establishment of a rhythmic continuity of general psychic interaction with the environment. Evident as a function productive of spontaneous reactions; the formation of habit-patterns; and the development of the *persona* as a habitual external attitude of convenience to meet the demands of society and convention.

(*e*) The function that possesses a powerful *emotional and erotic character*, especially for the male sex; and also possesses a *rationalizing character*, especially for the female sex. Strong likes and dislikes and prejudices can be attributed to this function.

(*f*) The function that has a significant and instinctive link with *ancestral patterns* built into the psychic structure and has a curious way of attracting the thoughts in the direction of the past.

Contributes largely to:

(*a*) The *inner personality*, described as the *anima* in a man and the *animus* in a woman; and also the *persona* or outer personality in both sexes. The Moon's association with these aspects of the psyche would appear to be that of a creative and actuating function of relationship between the persona and the inner personality. What Jung has defined as the "pregnant and creative qualities of the inner attitude"[6] can now be seen to be the source of those many traits astrologers have connected with the Moon for centuries, such as the feminine principle, maternal instincts, fertility. The anima and animus are a kind of bridge between the individual and the collective unconscious world, by which man and woman can learn to develop those qualities from within that are lacking in their outer personality.

(*b*) The *mind* (conscious psychological activity) and the growth and activity of the *ego*. In the sense that the persona is largely a representation of consciousness, and is a mediating function between the ego and the outer world, and the anima and animus mediate between the ego and the inner world.

Characteristic desire trends activated: Creativeness, protectiveness, productiveness, adaptation, tenacity, animation, spontaneity.

Potential root-traits motivated:

1. *Constructive*

Animation, sensitiveness, creativeness, impressionableness, imagination, domestication, prudence, sympathy, sociableness, protectiveness, tenacity, romanticizing, conscientiousness, affection, modesty, kindness, sentimentality, receptiveness and assimilation, intuitiveness, productiveness, good memory, adaptability, introspection and reflectiveness.

2. *Destructive*
Instability, unreliable, morbid sensitivity, frivolousness, too changeable and restless, moodiness, fussiness, touchiness, indecisiveness, prejudice, superstitious, clannishness, timidness, weak-willed, procrastination, easily influenced, apathetic, tendency to emotional outbursts, prone to fantasies.

Traditional association with: Liquids—especially water and milk, the sea and marine life, rain, humidity, moisture, serous surfaces, swamps, floods, rivers, oils, shipping, travel generally but especially voyages, females generally but especially the mother, family and home, servants, marriage, menstruation, gestation, maternal instincts, midwives, fertilization, fruitfulness, mediumship, nursing, fermentation, vessels in general—as receptacles, brewing and baking, property and place of residence, the land and crops, the general public, public commodities, dealings with the public, ordinary or common affairs of daily life, popularity, changes and fluctuations, rhythm.

Practical interpretation

The primary function of the Moon is *actuation*, the function necessary for bringing a psychic process into action. Therefore, if we find the Moon in a chart forms only one or two weak traditional aspects, or is totally unaspected, this suggests that the subject will have much difficulty bringing his ideas and plans to satisfactory fruition. There may be considerable inhibition, perhaps extreme sensitivity to the environment resulting in inability one way or another to adjust himself to or project himself into the environment with positive affects. He may be full of ideas, yet be unable to bring these to fruition without a great deal of effort. If the Sun, too, is weakly aspected or heavily afflicted there could be much psychological disturbance and difficulty in adapting and integrating himself to the world in general. It should be pointed out that it is not necessary for the Moon to contact the Sun within orb of a traditional aspect for the Moon to be an "actuating or animating" influence to the integrating processes of the Sun's function. The Moon's animating influence will be judged as potentially productive and strong, or otherwise, according to its relationship to the whole chart in terms of sign-placing and aspects or angularity. A heavily afflicted Moon by aspects will not necessarily be unproductive in terms of activity; indeed, it could function as an excessively stimulating factor (e.g. ☽ ☍ ♂ and □♃), but demanding the utmost self-control and restraint on the part of the individual concerned if he is to avoid conflict with others and dissipation or forceful application of his energies.

The Moon in our example chart is in Sagittarius, an outgoing and essentially extraverted mode of energy-release. This will tend to be the typical, spontaneous reaction of the subject to external life. But the square aspects to ♃ and ♄ will be likely to bring frustrations and disappointments and a possible resultant inversion of energy when under stress of longish periods of frustration and wasted effort. Inversion could develop into self-inhibiting modes of reaction (♄), or sudden extravagant or exaggerated expenditure of energy (♃) as the psychic processes seek a compensatory outlet for libido.

In terms of this function's contribution to the formation of habit-patterns, ☽□♄ is likely to make this subject easily susceptible to a compulsive development of *defensive* habit-patterns. At times this could appear to be a completely unconscious or instinctive avoidance of certain potentially difficult-to-cope-with or fear-provoking situations.

This function's contribution to the development of the *ego* (primarily through growth of consciousness represented by the *persona*), will be most significantly interpreted from the sign ♐, and aspects formed. These suggest the mode of energy-release, the likely stress, conflict and inhibitions, and the type of situations gravitated towards for the development of *conscious* experience of environment and self.

The Moon's function symbolizes the rhythmic ebb and flow of energy, especially in terms of the persona as mediator between the ego and the outside world, and in terms of the anima or animus which mediate between the ego and the collective unconscious. In our example case there could be difficulty in achieving a continuity of rhythmic energy exchanges between these psychic functions, due to the lack of a strong harmonious aspect with any other chart factor, and the existence of the uneasy aspects with ♃/♄. In terms of the persona or outer personality this might mean an uneasy self-consciousness; the temptation to sometimes exaggerate as an attitude of social convenience or to compensate for a lack of achievement in another direction; or a habitual shyness, resulting in the late development of an effective or reasonably socially-adjusted persona. As the subject of our example chart is a male, we might suggest that the Moon function's contribution to the type of *anima* he would possess could be that of typical feelings and an emotional nature that we would look for in a female with ♐ strong in her make-up.

NOTES

1. Carl G. Jung: *Symbols of Transformation*, p. 261 (Routledge & Kegan Paul, London).
2. Jolan Jacobi: *The Psychology of Jung*, p. 45 (Routledge & Kegan Paul, London).
3. Carl G. Jung: *Psychology and Alchemy*, p. 41 (Routledge & Kegan Paul, London).
4. Carl G. Jung: *Two Essays on Analytical Psychology*, p. 240 (Routledge & Kegan Paul, London).
5. *Ibid.*, p. 173.
6. Carl G. Jung: *Psychological Types*, p. 596 (Routledge & Kegan Paul, London).

6 *Communication; Co-ordination; Evaluation*

We have seen in the previous chapter that the Sun represents a source of self-generating energy for regulating and maintaining equilibrium within the psyche; whilst the Moon represents a complementary process which provides the self-generating forces with active properties: a dual and symbolically masculine-feminine function for creating impulses of purposeful activity for the human psyche's unfoldment through interaction with its environment.

For man to realize his full potentialities of self-expression, to learn to recognize the unique qualities of his own nature, he must become *consciously involved* with his environment. He must establish *communication* with the external world, which demands successful *adaptation* and the ability to *co-ordinate* knowledge and experience, so that his active relationship with his environment is fully comprehensible. Inevitably he will realize that his own life and being is *interdependent* with the lives of his fellows. He cannot survive without the co-operation and sympathetic attachment with his fellow creatures. He learns to appreciate and thence to *evaluate* things and people, and his mental and feeling processes of communication and evaluation create new dimensions of experience and living.

In this present chapter we will see how astrological factors, the planets Mercury and Venus, appear to correlate with or symbolize the vital psychic functions of communication, co-ordination, and evaluation.

Mercury (☿)

Primary function: Communication and co-ordination.

Definition: To establish *communication* with the environment.

This is achieved (*a*) in terms of *conscious* activity through the mind and mental processes, and (*b*) through nervous impulses and responses. Through the instruments of brain and central nervous system man is able to *co-ordinate* all nerve impulses and reflexes, all sensory information, and the complex patterns of intuitions, ideas and impressions derived from both inner unconscious sources and experience of his environment, into an intelligent projection of his own unique nature.

Further definitions:

(*a*) A need to store information and knowledge in the thinking areas of the brain and to weave these into the mind through *analysis and co-ordination*, for the appropriate opportunities for communication with the environment.

(*b*) A need to *adapt* oneself to the environment in terms of the conscious, nervous, and sensory faculties. Hence, related to the control of nervous energy, to the intelligible conveyance of thoughts through speech and writing, and to the means of interpreting experiences and learning from these.

(*c*) A need to develop *sociability*, for the exchange of ideas, the exercise of the mental faculties, debative intercourse, and transference of oneself through touch and sound and eyesight to other persons.

(*d*) A need to develop the *intellect* and intelligence, for studious pursuits and for teaching others.

(*e*) An important factor in regard to the desire to make *changes*, and to *transport* oneself physically or mentally.

Contributes largely to:

(*a*) The activity of the *mind* (conscious psychological activity). Here Mercury's contribution can be seen as the *process* by which man can *communicate* with his external world. It is the function through which he is able to register and interpret his experiences, to reason and debate, to project his thoughts and ideas into the world outside himself. In essence, it is the process of communication, and man's *need* to communicate with life outside himself, and the accompanying nervous and sensory involvement. It is the means by which the impulses for purposeful activity generated and actuated by the functions of Sun and Moon can be communicated beyond himself, and which contributes largely towards man being made conscious of these impulses.

(b) The growth of the *ego*, and essentially its means of conscious communication, and its means of conscious adaptation to the environment.

(c) The *inner personality*, comprising the *anima* in a man and the *animus* in a woman. But where the *mental* processes are concerned its contribution is most significantly directed towards the activity and rationalizing processes of the animus. Inevitably it must be associated with the exchanges between the inner personality and the outer personality (the *persona*), and provide the mental and nervous mobility and communicative ability of the persona.

Characteristic desire trends activated: Adaptability, mental exercise, versatility, communicativeness, co-ordination, information exchange, volatility.

Potential root-traits motivated:

1. *Constructive*
   Inquisitiveness, analytical ability, cleverness, skilfulness, studiousness, communicativeness, eloquence, good memory, technical ability, versatility, fluency, lucidity, adaptability, wittiness, debativeness, volatility, perceptiveness, shrewdness.

2. *Destructive*
   Restlessness, nervousness, criticalness, cunning, meddlesomeness, carelessness, clumsiness, forgetfulness, indecisiveness, unreliability, excitableness, inconstancy, worrisomeness, over-talkativeness.

Traditional association with: Literary works, publishing, printing, correspondence, the Press, advertising, messengers, teaching and education, study, the intelligentsia, communications generally, the postal services, transport generally, commerce, trading, merchandise, agents, changes, travel, markets, mathematics, libraries.

Practical interpretation

Mercury represents a survival-need for man to *communicate* with his fellows and to *adapt* himself intelligently to his environment. If we refer to the chart on page 65 we will see just how important communication and adaptation will be for the subject concerned. Not only because Mercury's particular relationship to the whole chart makes him more than normally vulnerable to external demands and pressures affecting the nervous and mental systems, but also because such an abundance of psychic energy will be readily available for release through this function. Mercury is conjunction to the Ascendant and is one of the strongest aspected factors in the chart. With Scorpio rising, and its co-ruler Mars conjunction Venus and opposition Uranus, and its other co-ruler Pluto very strongly aspected and square Sun, this man will need to learn to keep his emotions well controlled. The feelings will be deep and intense. Thus, Mercury rising in the chart, and its critical widespread links with so many other factors, suggests a person whose high sensitivity will be reflected in quick nervous reactions to external stimuli and pressures, and spontaneous feeling-reactions. Emotional stresses and intensity of feeling will tend to influence or to colour the mental processes; and, similarly, the natural intensity of mental activity will tend to draw on the feelings (evaluation) and emotional energies.

Mental pursuits and exercise will be an important need for this individual, and though intellectual subjects will interest and fascinate him, this is not the chart of an intellectual *type*—the psyche has the potential to generate such an exuberance of *feeling* (☿ ASC/♏︎, ♀☌ ♂, ♆ strong, ☽♐︎).

A high degree of sensitivity to the environment (☿☌ ASC, ☽□♄, ♆☌ MC) suggests continual difficulties and tensions in his efforts to establish and maintain satisfactory adaptation to external conditions. But this sensitivity is also a key to a potentially very keen perceptiveness.

Mercury's placing in the example chart shows a great need for sociability, though disappointments and frustrations could be experienced in this direction (☽□♄, ♀☌ ☍♅), and ☿□♆ suggests likely attraction to unorthodox experiences for sensory arousal and experimentation, where commonsense would be required to avoid resultant trouble and mental strain.

Venus (♀)

Primary function: Feeling-evaluation; sense of interdependence.

Definition: To develop *interdependent relationships* with other persons and environmental factors, based on *evaluation* through the feelings as opposed to a rational judgement by the mental faculties.

Further definitions:

(a) This is a function totally concerned with the *feelings* or the virtual lack of feeling. Inevitably mental and nervous processes must be involved in the transmission and expression of feeling, as also on occasions the sensory organs. But the significant point is that any interpretation of Venus in psychological terms *must* refer to traits whose essential content or motive force is that of *feeling* and not of purely mental and intellectual processes.

(b) A need to *relate* oneself to others; to form relationships, attachments; or even to be compelled or attracted to encounter apparent disharmonious personal contacts. Whatever the relationships sought or forged, the motive power behind the Venus function involved will be the need to relate oneself to others and to evaluate the experience through the feelings.

(c) A need to develop *co-operational patterns* of behaviour with others: unity of purpose, co-operation, sympathy, empathy —promoted consciously or not by the necessity of *interdependence*. A need to develop *sociability*, the tendency to behave socially, to seek company, and to participate eagerly in group activities.

(d) A need to *unite or resolve opposites*, in a seeking for development through complementary values. A seeking to harmonize, balance, unify, smooth out the rough and the discordant, and create cohesion, rhythm and equilibrium.

(e) A *centripetal* process, an essentially inner and subjective experience. The urge and power to *attract*. A need to realize the very quintessence of an experience and to transmute this into feeling-evaluation.

(*f*) Represents the *feminine impulse* in both sexes. It is more than the physical aspect of a sexual relationship: it is the desire to unite opposites, the power behind loving, need for affection. It is the feeling within the creative impulse: the essence of creativity.

(*g*) A need *to appreciate and to be appreciated*; a need to cherish a thing or person; the desire to reduce friction and disharmony between oneself and the environment to a minimum; a need for aesthetic enjoyment of beauty in nature and art, and for aesthetic preferences for symmetry, proportion, and balance.

Contributes largely to:

(*a*) The development of the *ego*. Particularly as the Venus function's feeling-nature is primarily a process that takes place between the ego and a given content, in the sense that the process imparts to the content a distinct *value* in terms of acceptance or rejection, like or dislike.

(*b*) Probably a significant aspect of the *anima* within a man, in terms of his own latent feminine traits, and the archetypal image he carries within himself (mostly unconscious) of the ideal woman he will instinctively seek in his experiences of women. Likewise, this function could form a significant aspect of the *persona* of a woman, but only in terms of the feeling content, and its process of evaluation which would aid the selection of the appropriate mode of adaptation and response to the environment. We recall that the persona is an attitude of convenience between the individual consciousness and society.

(*c*) The need to relate and to unite oneself with others, which, to be genuine, and to satisfy a fundamental need, spiritually or biologically, must involve the *feeling-nature,* as a basic expression of the psyche as a whole.

Characteristic desire trends activated: Co-operation, harmony, sympathy, compromise, creativeness, artistry, idealism, aestheticism.

Potential root-traits motivated:

1. *Constructive*

   Co-operation, artistry, cheerfulness, kindness, sympathy, humaneness, compassion, affectionateness, sociability, amorousness, refinement, idealism, chasteness, gentleness, amicableness, placidness, tactfulness, passiveness, empathy, aestheticism.

2. *Destructive*

   Unco-operativeness, self-indulgence, indolence, immorality, disorderliness, boorishness, thoughtlessness, over-sensuousness, tactlessness, timidness, vanity, lustfulness.

Traditional association with: Love and romance, marriage, sociability, love affairs, sensuality, sexual intercourse, beauty, pleasures, entertainment, social functions, festivities, the arts, dancing, rhythm, harmony, money, beautiful possessions, females generally, sugars and spices, the significator of victory in war, trades and industries catering mainly for women (such as cosmetics and jewellery).

Practical interpretation

Venus is associated with the function in man that needs to give a distinct *value* to a thing, a person, or a situation, through the *feelings*. When this planet is prominent in a chart we can expect the feelings to be strongly evident in the subject's self-expression and disposition. This we can judge to be the case with the subject of the example chart on page 65. Venus is ruler of Libra (♎), the sign occupied by the Sun; and is conjunction Mars (co-ruler of Scorpio-Ascendant), opposition Uranus, sextile Mercury and Pluto.

This man should tend to develop keen personal values and therefore be sensitive and discriminating (♀♍) in the formation of close relationships and in his choice of involvement with his environment.

A compulsive and dominating feature of archetypal influence will be the need for him to experience life and other people on an *intimate* basis—the need to know and understand any object or situation beyond their face-value, to penetrate to the core of a thing, to uncover, analyse, and thus to *relate* one thing to another and to himself. The Venus function will be a prominent and active influence in this respect.

There is little doubt that the sexual drive will be powerfully responded to with the feelings and emotions readily activated as indicated by ASC-♏, (♀ ☌ ♂) ☍♅ in 5th house. The need to develop *interdependent relationships* will be a vital motivation to this person's choice of action. Though inhibition or frustration (☽□♄) may prevent or delay a successful fulfilment of this drive.

7 Self-Projection; Expansion; Control

The individual man, physically detached from all others of his kind, is nevertheless inseparably linked with the whole of humanity through the roots of his own psyche which grow out of the collective unconscious—that boundless realm containing the entire history of mankind and from which all consciousness and impulses for activity emerge. Man experiences collectively his inherited patterns of instinctive behaviour, bequeathed to him by his ancestors through their repetitive experiences shaping his brain and nerve structures. Yet as individual consciousness arises out of the mysterious undercurrents of the unconscious, man, true to his ever-questing nature, must strive to realize himself as unique from the rest of mankind. To realize this as truth, he establishes communication with his environment through conscious involvement and adaptation; learning to co-ordinate his faculties; begrudgingly perhaps accepting the interdependence of all human creatures; and furthering his claims for uniqueness by developing an ability to evaluate his relationship with objects and situations of his environment. By conscious awareness and discrimination he creates new dimensions of experience and living.

He has reached the stage, with new dimensions of experience challenging him to further prove his uniqueness of being, where he must *project* himself actively and energetically into the external world. He must objectively influence and master his environment, impress his signature upon all that he encounters. Achievement and conquest through self-directed initiative and enterprise demands and creates fresh opportunities for self-expression. Thus, new horizons appear before him with the *expansion* of his consciousness and the widening of his field of activity, and he finds himself participating deeper and deeper in experience of life and the surging, outward flow of his own energy could threaten to engulf him or evaporate him, and hence his identity and claim for uniqueness be lost for ever. Energy, actively projected into ever-expanding fields of exploration, needs to be *controlled* and regulated by *formative processes* and structural limits, so that its potential can be fully realized.

In this present chapter we will see how astrological factors, the planets Mars, Jupiter and Saturn, appear to correlate with or symbolize the vital psychic functions of self-projection, self-expansion, and self-control.

Mars (♂)

Primary function: Self-projection; energetic emotional activity.

Definition: To develop a system of *energetic and active self-projection*, as a means of objectively influencing or mastering the environment, or for defence of the organism.

Further definitions:

(*a*) A *centrifugal* process, energy flowing outwards.

(*b*) A need to be *self-assertive*, to take the initiative, to be enterprising, objective, and to pioneer new ventures.

(*c*) Associated with the *ascendancy trait*: a tendency to be masterful in any situation, whether involving other people or not; to dominate, to show superior strength.

(*d*) Represents the *masculine impulse* in both sexes. In the *sex drive* it is essentially the physical desire and passion for sensual gratification, and the masculine need to thrust, to penetrate, to eject emotional energy and seed.

(*e*) All drives associated with this function are inevitably accompanied by *emotion*. Emotion is the way the body feels when it is prepared or stimulated for particular action or reaction. Emotion is *personal involvement* in an experience —the more intimate the involvement, the more intense the emotion, and involvement stimulates self-projective activity. Emotion serves to sustain, and in its less violent form, to facilitate action.

(*f*) A need to *encounter* life outside oneself; to respond to the challenge of the environment in terms of combat and resistance.

(g) A need to preserve the self as a *separate organism*, to achieve and maintain one's independence, and express singleness of purpose in action.

(h) A need for *aggressive action*: to influence the environment, direct the course of one's life, to attack problems, master a subject of interest, to survive by attack or defence.

Contributes largely to:

(a) The development of the *ego*, in terms of the self-projective drives which the Mars' function responds to.

(b) Probably a significant aspect of the *animus* within a woman, in terms of her own latent masculine traits, and the archetypal image she carries within herself (mostly unconscious) of the ideal man she will instinctively seek in her experiences of men. Likewise, this function could form a significant aspect of the *persona* of a man, providing objectivity and assertiveness in his compromising adjustment to the demands of society and convention.

Characteristic desire trends activated: Energetic activity, initiative, self-assertion, enterprise, combativeness, aggressiveness, ambition, independence, forcefulness.

Potential root-traits motivated:

1. *Constructive*
   Activeness, courageousness, venturesomeness, pioneering, independence, ambition, enterprise, self-assertion, decisiveness, competitiveness, persuasiveness, spontaneity, adventuresomeness.

2. *Destructive*
   Aggressiveness, forcefulness, coarseness, impulsiveness, impatience, sensuousness, pugnacity, brazenness, recklessness, wilfulness, fieriness, self-centredness, foolhardiness, brusqueness, quarrelsomeness, dominance, impetuousness, non-co-operation, excitableness, lustfulness, militance, mischievousness, intolerance.

Traditional association with: Energy, activity, passion, fire, fevers, burns, cuts, scalds, war, strife, heat, bloodshed, violence, accidents, murder, arsony, the Armed Services, masculinity, munitions, slaughter-houses; all engineering and constructional industries; industries dependent upon machinery, iron, steel, or furnace-heating; pungent odours, hot acids, burning astringents; manual skill and technical ability—able to use tools and instruments of all types for the utilization of energy; sexual desire; dispersion.

Practical interpretation

In looking to Mars in a chart we are considering the person's potential ability for *projecting* himself energetically and actively. The sign that Mars occupies and the aspects it forms with other planets will suggest the mode of energy-release, typical behaviour and responses in which the Mars-function will be involved, the likelihood of too much self-assertion or aggression and resultant conflict with others, or a probable "inhibited Mars-function" which suggests lack of assertiveness, timidity, or a neurotic tendency.

The subject of the chart on page 65 has Mars as co-ruler with Pluto of the rising sign Scorpio. The main complex is ♂(☌ ♀ in ♍) ☍♅. Energy will tend to be channelled in precise, orderly, meticulous ways (♂♍), and likely artistic/ creative impulses (♂☌ ♀, ☉♎) would attract much energetic attention and a possible flair for originality (♂ ☍♅).

It would be vital that the subject has a satisfactory outlet for sexual energy and expression (♂☌ ♀☍♅; ♂ ruler of ♏- ASC), though problems or frustrated expression in this direction could be sublimated, if only temporarily, through mental channels (♂✶ both the ☿ and ♇ points of the Grand Trine involving ☿ ♇♅).

With ♂☌ ♀ (♀ ruler of ♎, the Sun-sign) this subject's need for friendship (especially where emotion and feeling can be spontaneously expressed, as with the opposite sex) will be a vitally important factor for personal happiness and self-fulfilment. ♀♂ ☍♅ suggests risk of sudden terminations of emotional ties and friendships, as well as an attraction for unorthodox relationships and a potential flavour for just plain bawdy sexual experimentation!

The example chart does not indicate a male subject whose Mars-function related to the overall chart-pattern shows an essentially aggressive or even an actively self-assertive nature. This is because ☉♎ suggests a compromising, friendly, easy-going basic desire trend, whilst ☉ in 12th house and ☽□♄ point to probable inhibitive-patterns and resultant sensitivity to self-exposure or the risk of open conflict with others. But aggressive and assertive instincts *must* have outlets, for health's sake, as well as for balancing purposes within the psyche, and these outlets could be evident on occasions, probably at times of prolonged frustration or provocation, in the form of sudden explosive, emotionally-charged outbursts (☉□ ♇, ♂♂♅) which the subject may naturally claim to be justified reactions (☉♎: I don't *want* to fight you, but you force me to do so!)

Jupiter (♃)

Primary function: Self-expansion.

Definition: to achieve *expansion* of the consciousness through knowledge, study, understanding; and improvement of one's material affairs through opportunist and mature handling of matters.

Further definitions:

(*a*) A need to improve oneself mentally and emotionally, so that *one's character grows*, *matures* and understanding of life broadens, that the *right action* and decisions are taken.

(*b*) A need to *improve one's status* and to acquire the best things in life. To *progress*; to seize *opportunities*; to develop the ability to gain an *advantage* over others—not in the sense of feeling superior or more powerful, but so that one is *responsible* only to oneself and to one's *conscience*.

(*c*) A need to *enrich* one's life and being by responsible, conscientious, just, and lawful means.

(*d*) A need to achieve *increase* mentally, materially, and spiritually—not for the acquiring and hoarding of the rewards of one's efforts, but to *spread* one's gains among others for their benefit also.

(*e*) A need to be *liberal*, generous, open-minded, philosophical.

(*f*) A need to be aware of one's *conscience*, manifesting as applying justice with mercy, an inner sense of law, order, morals, religious conviction, and a desire to protect, heal, and preserve where needed.

(*g*) A need for *deeper participation* in experience: through self-exploration; through exploring new horizons and situations, mentally and physically; and by gaining broader understanding through study and reasoned judgement.

(*h*) A need to achieve *compensation* for inadequacies or failures elsewhere in the organism, implying that this function represents the "regulator of uniform yet progressive growth".

(*i*) A need to *"look to the future"*, in terms of expansion, opportunity, advancement, progress, improvement, and the seeking for new horizons of experience. Hence, Jupiter's connection with prophets and seers.

Contributes largely to:

(*a*) The unfoldment of the *self*, in terms of the Jupiter-function's urge for expansion, improvement, self-exploration, compensatory adjustments, and its significant association with conscience.

(*b*) The process of *individuation*: the development of the individual as a differentiated being from the general, an extension of the sphere of consciousness, an enriching of the conscious psychological life.

Characteristic desire trends activated: Self-expansion, opportunism, conscientiousness, generosity, justice, exploration, progressiveness, studiousness, philosophizing, protectiveness (towards others).

Potential root-traits motivated:

1. *Constructive*
Opportunism, sociableness, moderateness, idealism, reasonability, progressiveness, mindfulness of others, benevolence, charitableness, hospitality, sincerity, compassion, justness, trustworthiness, impartiality, optimism, buoyancy, joviality, conscientiousness, protectiveness, broad-mindedness, philosophizing, serenity, devotion.

2. *Destructive*
Extravagance, restlessness, recklessness, conceit, procrastination, over-exuberance, lawlessness, exaggerativeness, snobbishness, self-righteousness, pretentiousness, fanaticism, ill-judgement, dissipation, exhibitionism, hypocriticalness, dishonesty, self-indulgence, compulsive social-climbing, over-extension of oneself.

Traditional association with: Religion and the clergy, philosophy, higher education, study, the Law and legalities, guardianship, professions generally, dignitaries, sport—especially horse-racing and hunting and athletics, gambling, speculative ventures, banking and the Stock Market, abundance, development, growth, supply, surplus, wealth, financial dealings, affluence, luxury, profit, prosperity, good fortune, good favour, honours, prestige, opportunity, success, optimism, happiness, protection, philanthropy, luck, physicians, foreign affairs, distant travel, gluttony, obesity, wholesomeness, inflation, insurance, judgement, fulfilment, devotion, prodigality.

Practical interpretation

The most significant key to the interpretation of a person's potential capacity for *self-expansion* and deeper and *successful participation* in life is that of Jupiter in the birth-chart.

In the example chart on page 65 we find Jupiter in Libra (♎), which indicates that the archetypal compulsion associated with Jupiter will tend to make the subject's Sun-sign Libran traits extremely prominent and spontaneous. This also implies that it will be through the basic Libran mode of reaction and predisposing attitude that he will most naturally realize the best opportunities for expansion—mentally, and also in terms of his material needs and objectives. It is a curious fact of life, that the prominent features in a chart (and therefore in one's make-up) appear to 'attract' or to help create important situations and environmental conditions throughout the life. In our example case we should find that the Libran traits will tend to attract or to help create environmental conditions which should prove to be aptly appropriate for furthering the development of these traits, and for providing them with fuller scope for expression. Thus, he will probably find that he is brought into significant and also intimate relationships with certain individuals who would seem to dramatically test his innate desire for harmony and co-operation with his fellows. And if he can succeed in winning them over to his Libran friendliness the placing of Jupiter in Libra should reward him with deeply happy experiences through which his life and his conscious awareness to others will open to new and challenging horizons for further growth and benefits.

However, ♃ is ☌♄, and both planets are □☽. Here is a pointer to potential unhappiness and frustration. ♃ and ♄ are opposites: expansion *v* limitation. Dependent upon circumstances and the subject's ability and strength of will to master these two opposing forces and their aggravating tensions within his psyche, so could these prove ultimately beneficial: ♄ providing a practical framework (mentally conceived) for the controlled release of the energies of Jupiter-inspired motives; ♃ encouraging optimism and a philosophical attitude towards the acceptance and eventual overcoming of Saturnian restriction and denial. Whilst the psychic function symbolized by the Moon, stimulated and sensitized by the conflicts generated by the □ aspects, would provide actuation to the ♃-♄ complementary impulses.

This has been very true in this man's case. Bitter disharmony between the parents in the childhood home tended to make even more acute the innate sensitivity of the nature, resulting in eventual inhibition (through shyness and lack of timely encouragement) of the normal Sagittarian outgoing traits. This inhibitive influence tended to involve the subject in countless embarrassing and unhappy experiences as he grew up, with the accumulative effect of causing him to build defensive and withdrawal systems to avoid further unhappiness. He chose to avoid difficult situations rather than to meet their challenge. But out of this pattern of withdrawal and evasion, and as a direct result of it in the form of Jupiterian *compensation*, he developed the studious and analytical side of his nature which gave him the eventual opportunity to build a successful career. A career which demanded the type of concentration and intense application of energies that he was able to give to the specialist nature of the work. The Moon has actuated the ♍︎≏♐︎ traits, ideally needed in his role as a teacher and where an understanding of the basic principles of psychology is required. But an afflicting Saturn seems to always demand a sacrifice and to leave a scar as a permanent reminder of one's encounters with this severely testing archetype. In this subject's case, a broken marriage.

Yet, with ☉ and ♃ in ≏ the future can still bring an ideal partnership, the potential for realizing the opportunity being contained in the psyche, and the self that much the wiser for its hard and disappointing experiences.

Just as no birth-chart is ever too severely afflicted for there to be no relief or release from troubles and suffering, so too are there always the opportunities for the worst afflicted psyche to realize some form of satisfying compensation. Simply because every psyche, every human being, has the potential to draw on the energies of the archetype symbolized by ♃, and to interpret its personal meaning for one's self-realization and growth.

Saturn (♄)

Primary function: Self-control and formative processes.

Definition: To develop *self-control* through formative processes requiring a sense of method and purpose, self-reliance and discipline, realistic and constructive thinking.

Further definitions:

(*a*) A need to formulate *constructive material values*, and develop a realistic and practical attitude to life.

(*b*) A need to *think clearly*, logically; to construct concrete thought-patterns; to give *practical and purposeful* form to ideas; to plan; to be accurate and distinct in one's self-expression.

(*c*) A need to be *resourceful and economical* and able to *concentrate* energy and thought on a selected object or goal; to consolidate and conserve.

(*d*) A need to be conscious of and able to develop necessary *boundaries or structural limits*, for regulating or controlling energy and growth.

(e) A need to be *serious and reflective* when occasions demand; to develop a sense of *duty and responsibility* towards one's fellows.

(f) The function that produces a sense of *personal isolation*, separateness, aloneness from all other forms of life, and a sense of personal inadequacy.

(g) A need for *self-denial* or sacrifice; for self-restraint.

(h) A need for *stability and perseverance*; and the ability for sustained, monotonous, laborious work requiring patience and self-discipline.

(i) The function that develops an attitude towards *religion* of dedication to correct form, to a rigid code of conduct, elaborate rites and ceremonies, within a religious order, rather than a spirit of heartfelt devotion and humility.

(j) A need to construct a system for *protection* of the organism, in terms of instinctive defence tactics against environmental pressures and assault, rather than attack. Hence, potential defence and withdrawal mechanisms, inhibitive-patterns, defensive-avoidance reactions.

Contributes largely to:

(a) The development of the *self*. Particularly in terms of the Saturn-function's compulsive insistence on the development of self-consciousness through: logical, common sense, and contemplative thinking; realistic, responsible and practical behaviour; the practice of self-restraint and self-reliance.

(b) The *ego*, also in terms of the Saturn-function's emphasis on the above controlled development of self-consciousness, and, too, related to the Saturn-function's production of a sense of separateness or awareness of one's uniqueness from all other human beings.

Characteristic desire trends activated: Self-consciousness, self-control, self-reliance and discipline, practicality, resourcefulness, caution and restraint, conservation, self-protection.

Potential root-traits motivated:

1. *Constructive*
Self-reliance, self-discipline, seriousness, profundity, patience, prudence, cautiousness, reliableness, organizing and

executive ability, preciseness, resoluteness, contemplation, reserve, punctuality, perseverance, industriousness, thoroughness, persistence, soberness, faithfulness, dutiful- ness, conservatism, introspection, conscientiousness, thrifti- ness, endurability, self-restraint, the need to be methodical, calculating and analytical.

2. *Destructive*
Unreliability, bigotedness, scepticism, secretiveness, sus- piciousness, pessimism, melancholia, depressiveness, fatal- ism, censorious, frigidity, mistrustfulness, stubbornness, apprehensiveness, shyness, nervousness, narrow-mindedness, self-repression, heartlessness, incompetence, touchiness, coldness of feelings, maliciousness, over-materialistic.

Traditional association with: Coldness, frigidness, refrigeration, limitation, frustration, restriction, obstruction, delays, retarda- tion, coagulation, congealment, crystallization, confinement, coherence, fixation, enchainment, imprisonment, concretion, consolidation, cement, weightiness, earthiness, atrophy, decay, death, deterioration, deficiency, losses, famine, burial grounds, graves and tombs, caves, chronic ailments, long illness, suffer- ing, filtering processes, mill-stones, economy, habits, old age, time, weights and measures, mathematics, framework, struc- ture, form, routine, monotony, drudgery, hard work, sorrow, adversity, fatalities, fatalism, depression, melancholy, mis- fortunes, failure, poverty, bankruptcy, demotion, retributive justice, impediments, defects, budgeting, burdens, debts, responsibility, falls, bruises, broken bones, fear, foreboding, darkness, dark things and places, secrecy, property, mining, coal, agriculture and land, the past, lead.

Practical interpretation
Of all the planets probably Saturn is the easiest to understand in terms of related human behaviour and the ills and afflictions that can befall man. Yet it can be far from easy to accurately interpret from a birth-chart the potentially dominant reactions of the individual to the Saturn-function in his own personal and unique case.
One needs to assess from the whole chart-pattern the

probable *sensitivity* of the subject to the strains and stresses and inhibiting pressures that can be encountered through environmental conditions, as a result of the Saturn-related archetypal forces working through mankind collectively, and at given critical times through the individual personally. In short, how sensitive is he to stress through frustration and heavy afflictions?

In the case of the subject whose chart is shown on page 65, it is apparent that he will be extremely sensitive to Saturn-type afflictions ($\mathbb{D}\square\hbar$, $\odot\simeq$, $\mathbb{\xi}$ rising in $\mathbb{m}$, and $\square\Psi$/MC, $\mathbb{Q}\mathbb{\delta}\mathbb{\delta}\mathbb{\delta}\mathbb{\%}$). The critical formula for depressive reactions is $\mathbb{D}\square\hbar$ (intensified by $\mathbb{D}\square\mathbb{2}\mathbb{L}$ ($\mathbb{\delta}\hbar$), and any frustrating or binding affects on the freedom-seeking Sagittarian-Moon). $\mathbb{\xi}$ rising and being $\square$ the angular Ψ suggests that afflictions/conflicts will tend to aggravate and excite nervous reactions, and that mental and emotional sensitivity to external and depressive pressures could be a great trial.

$\odot\mathbb{2}\mathbb{L}$ in $\simeq$, and the potential depth of reasoning ability and stamina of $\mathbb{\xi}$ and $\mathbb{m}$, rising, are probable key factors for the achievement of a balanced and sensible resolving of problems associated with the Saturn-archetype's manifestations.

Jung speaks of the "daemonic qualities and projections" and the "irrational elfin nature" of the *anima* in a man, which is the archetype largely responsible for his compelling searchings for the ideal woman to complement his own predominant masculine nature. The anima seems to be especially associated with the Moon-function in a man. $\hbar\square\mathbb{D}$ suggests difficulties in terms of frustration and disappointment, and periods of irrational behaviour, where the women in the life of our example male-subject are concerned. Indeed, $\hbar\square\mathbb{D}$ combined with $\mathbb{\xi}\square\Psi$ and $\mathbb{Q}$ ($\mathbb{\delta}\mathbb{\delta}$) $\mathbb{\delta}\mathbb{\%}$, indicate that this subject can be easily influenced by the opposite sex.

It is of great value, through astrology, to be aware of our *personal limitations*. Various factors in the birth-chart can indicate what these probably are. Saturn's placing in our chart will, of course, be a prime pointer to the types and the severity of experiences that could impose frustrations and limitations upon us, as well as suggesting where our psyche could be particularly vulnerable to stress. But we must not paint the

Saturn-correlated archetype's influence on our lives too black, nor think it can only bring limitation and unhappiness. It is far preferable to think of this function within our psyche as being essential for helping us to develop self-control through the formative processes we have already defined.

8 Deviation; Refinement; Transformation

In the previous three chapters we have seen how the Sun, Moon, and five of the planets are correlated symbolically with various dynamic aspects of the human psyche. When a particular situation, apprehension, or need in the life of an individual human being occurs and corresponds to a given archetype (or pattern of instinctual behaviour), that archetype or basic and unconsciously-formed behavioural-response becomes activated. The activated unconscious content manifests in typical thought, feeling or emotional processes of response to the environment or to the object of stimulation. Or, put in another way, a man or a woman may think that *they* decide exactly how they should respond to a given situation, whereas their responses are largely conditioned and determined by inherited patterns of instinctual emotional and mental behaviour.

But the more consciously-evolved a man becomes, so will he have increasing power and intelligence to *freely* express himself through the initial energy and guiding impulse of the archetypes of the unconscious.

Man, consciously or unconsciously orientating towards self-realization, develops his faculties of communication and adaptation as he interacts with his environment. He is forced to acknowledge or he welcomes the fact of his natural interdependence with others of his kind. By discrimination and evaluation he learns to create new dimensions of experience which challenge his self-projective powers and initiative. His life and his consciousness expand towards new horizons which inspire him to participate ever deeper in the complex process of living. He learns to control and to regulate his expenditure of energy and passion, to devise inhibiting codes of conduct, to invent authoritative systems and structures for keeping things and people within specified boundaries.

But natural man, dynamic psyche, knows no boundaries, no limits to the potentialities of self-expression and creative energy-release. Inevitably a part of man must seek to *deviate* from the normal or the conventional forms of expression, to be original, to experiment with totally new ideas, and to achieve this originality through independent and unrestricted and unconditional activity. In time the unconventional becomes the conventional, deviation leads to creative genius or to destructive anarchy or perversion. Life, to fulfil the perfection of the initial impulse of creation, must realize perfection in its every manifestation. The archetype of perfection demands continuous improvement and *refinement* of human expression. Deviation, originality, invention, improvement and refinement create new forms and new values and ultimately a *transformation* in the individual or the collective organism. A new cycle of self-realization begins, a new chapter of experience. The eternal cycle of elimination and renewal, death and rebirth, in the tortuous execution of the original life-impulse unfolding its mystery and purpose.

In this present chapter we will see how astrological factors, the planets Uranus, Neptune and Pluto, appear to correlate with or symbolize the vital psychic functions of deviation, refinement, and transformation.

Uranus (♅)

Primary function: Deviation from the normal.

Definition: To develop *independence, originality* of self-expression, *inventive* impulses, by following natural innate deviations from the normal growth-patterns and from the normal expected responses to the environment.

Further definitions:

(a) A need to *deviate* from the normal anticipated course of behaviour or of organic development, for the creation of entirely new forms of life-expression—psychologically, or involving environmental factors.

(b) A need to justify oneself in terms of *uniqueness* from all other beings; hence, manifesting in desire for independence, unconventional   behaviour-patterns,   freedom-seeking impulses, inventiveness, originality, creative inspiration, experimentation, unrestricted and unconditional self-expression.

(c) A need to *reform* or remodel outworn or limiting or retarding patterns and structures and formulae. Often manifesting negatively as drastic or destructive rejection of the old or the long-established and traditional structures of society, such as through personal rebellion or activated by widespread anarchistic demonstrations.

(d) The function that tends to *break down inhibitions* and thereby excite more natural freedom and healthier participation in sexual relationships; or the involvement in perverted sex-play, homosexuality, Lesbianism, or in fanatical or eccentric or freakish forms of anti-social behaviour—or simply a need to demonstrate deviational tendencies by peculiar yet inoffensive behaviour.

(e) The function that tends to produce *dramatic* and *disruptive* behaviour in the individual, which often causes equally dramatic and disruptive repercussions within his own area of society, or as a severing of matrimonial or other personal or business relationships.

(f) A need to introduce *sudden, unplanned changes* into one's pattern of life-activities.

(g) The function that can produce a dramatic flash of *genius*.

Contributes largely to:

(a) The expression of the *mind* (conscious psychological and mental activity). Especially in terms of wilful thinking, and abnormal, original, inventive, creative, and unusual thought-processes.

(b) The activity and unfoldment of the *inner personality* (the *anima* of a man, and the *animus* of a woman). In the sense that this inner personality would be likely to be purposefully involved in any deviations from the normal attitude of the outer personality. Such manifestations involving the anima and animus could be especially evident when the individual sheds an inhibition or two by wilfully disregarding demands made by convention upon his outer personality.

Characteristic desire trends activated: Independence, originality, inventiveness, curiosity, unconventionality, rebelliousness, idealism.

Potential root-traits motivated:

1. *Constructive*

   Originality, inventiveness, unconventionality, progressiveness, independence, intuitiveness, outspokenness, experimentation, creativeness, urge for reformative or pioneering activity.

2. *Destructive*

   Eccentricity, erraticalness, fanaticism, freakish abnormality, intolerance, impatience, brusqueness, aggressiveness, perversity, anarchism, irresponsibleness, licentiousness, autocracy, dictatorialness, ruthlessness, unreliableness, wilfulness, explosiveness, hatred of control, sensitivity to slights, extreme dislikes, urge to shock others.

Traditional association with: The unusual, the unorthodox and unconventional; science and anything connected with electronics or electricity, radio and television, aeronautics; invention, experimentation, originality, genius, curiosity, novelty, eccentricity, the grotesque, deformities, freaks, abnormality, premature occurrences, the unexpected and the unplanned, sudden and disruptive happenings, sudden changes, anarchism, revolution, upheaval, the unpredictable, dramatic and drastic happenings, surprises, shocks, explosions; catastrophes such as earthquakes and volcanic eruptions; accidents, suicides, convulsions and spasms, divorce, separation, estrangement, sudden broken ties, exiles, insecurity, ups and downs in life, sudden changes of fortune, strikes and rioting, liberty, freedom, independence, emancipation, occultism, civic bodies, societies and associations, radio-active metals and chemicals.

Practical interpretation

The primary function symbolized by Uranus is that of *deviation from the normal*. If one reads the definitions I have given for this function in man, one can clearly see how the various basic drives (such as creativeness, need for reformative activity, the urge to be uninhibited and independent of others) each has this central motive: to act and behave in an original manner, free from any need or obligation to conform to convention or tradition or to the influence of others. This is not a desire to simply be different *for the sake of* being different, actuated perhaps from sheer boredom or frustration. This is a vital need in man. The need to deviate in one's self-expression or course of action in an original and essentially self-determined manner. It is a voluntary departure from the intended or conventionally accepted course. When we respond to this Uranus-function's compulsive influence through our own personal links with the unconscious we usually do so spontaneously or with such suddenness that we ourselves are probably surprised— apart from the disruptive and dramatic effects upon other people concerned!

Unfortunately, and due mainly to the highly complex structure of civilized society and its constant pressures and demands which inhibit most of our natural instincts, we may rarely react to any major drive in a purely individual manner. Thus, we should find that few of us are able to fulfil the needs and purpose of the Uranus-function, and that mostly when we permit ourselves to respond to its promptings it is to behave in a very odd and unorthodox form, or perversely, or in a dramatically self-willed or rebellious manner. We feel the compulsion, but we cannot interpret its meaning, its essential need.

When Uranus is strong or significantly placed in a birth-chart (perhaps involved in several major aspects and/or conjunction an angle) we will find that the subject concerned tends to exhibit behaviour or is periodically "caught up in" dramatic and disruptive circumstances typical of that function or planet's symbology.

The example chart on page 65 shows Uranus strongly placed by aspects, indicative of this man's life and thought-patterns and motives being affected considerably by the archetypes correlated with this planet. This has been very true. So much of his compulsive and also consciously-sought attraction to the unconventional and to the unusual in life can be attributed to his readiness to express and experience this deep-rooted functional need. ♅ △ ☿ suggests potential ability to communicate original ideas and to seek mental exercise and analysis of unorthodox subjects. ♅△♇ points to possible major transformations to his life-pattern as a result of this need to deviate from a normal and expected course in life, with the opportunity to benefit and develop his character because of this. ♅♀♂ suggests dramatic ups and downs in regard to human relationships where the feelings and affections are necessarily involved, and the strong tendency to sexual experimentation. Freedom-seeking impulses will need to be recognized and compromised with, if not given completely uninhibited expression.

This Uranus-function within the psyche of man is an exciting feature to look for—if only we could learn to do this within ourselves, if only we had the courage and the understanding to freely express its ideas in terms of our own unique nature and by building these in practical form into our life-circumstances.

Neptune (♆)

Primary function: Refinement.

Definition: To achieve *refinement* in terms of *sensitivity* of feeling and *subtlety* of behaviour, *aesthetic* appreciation, *creative* fulfilment, based on *spiritual* and *humane* values as opposed to materialistic values; and with the need to continually elevate and revalue experience to achieve *perfection*.

Further definitions:

(a) A need to develop *sensitivity* of interpretation, judgement and appreciation, and of mental, emotional and physical responses. Hence, tending to be very impressionable and susceptible to environmental influences, and the nervous and emotional activity likely to be stimulated to an extreme pitch of sensitivity and excitement.

(b) The function that represents so much of the poet, the painter, the musician, the dreamer, and the inspired and dedicated religious leader in man.

(c) A need through the sensory mechanisms and the most sensitive perceptive faculties to seek experience *beyond and detached from all material form and structure*. Hence, potential vulnerability to various aspects of ecstasy, fantasy, escapism, self-deception, and mediumistic trance conditions.

(d) A need to experience an *ideal*. Hence, the likelihood of increasing dissatisfaction with commonplace day-by-day mundane affairs, and the potential vulnerability to glamour, sophistication, woolly-headedness, impracticality, daydreaming, and escapism through mysticism, drugs and sensational unconventional experiences.

(e) A need to bring oneself and one's environmental conditions to a more *perfect* state; to develop *culture, subtlety,* and to be free from rudeness, coarseness, or vulgarity.

(f) The function associated with the feeling-responses conducive to *inspiration*, and the *elevation* of oneself to a higher state of performance and accomplishment.

Contributes largely to:

(a) The development and fulfilment of the *self*, in terms of this Neptune-function's orientation of the psyche's conscious awareness towards the need for *refinement* and *perfection*.

(b) The expression of the *mind* (conscious psychological and mental activity), in terms of this Neptune-function's urge for cultural development and subtlety of thought.

Characteristic desire trends activated: Creativeness, sensitivity, imagination, aesthetic appreciation, humanitarianism, subtlety, idealism, romance, tenderness, religious devotion or a "universal love" embraced by mysticism, perfectionism.

Potential root-traits motivated:

1. *Constructive*
   Creativeness, aestheticism, subtlety, idealism, gentleness, impressionableness, humanitarianism, artistic sensitivity, refinement, elegance, virtuosity, perfectionism, devotionality.

2. *Destructive*
   Hyper-sensitiveness and touchiness, gullibility, woolly-headedness, vagueness, evasiveness, vacillation, impracticality, absent-mindedness, escapism; subject to hallucinations, hysteria, obsessional and intangible fears and phobias,

drug-addiction, perversion, suicidal tendencies, homo-sexuality, anxieties, premonitions, sensationalism; fraudu-lency, shyness, dishonesty, instability, nebulousness, worrisomeness, inefficiency, self-indulgence, dramatization, self-deception, eroticism; proneness to involvement in debauchery or scandal; subject to excessive emotion and to embarrassment; tendency for behaviour arising from inex-plicable motives, and to misunderstanding.

Traditional association with: Aestheticism, inspiration, mystic-ism, spiritualism, trance conditions, visions, magicians, secret societies, the hypnotist and the hypnotized, the sea and marine life generally, submarines, fishing industry, divers, oil, ether, intoxicating beverages, drugs, anaesthetics, gases, inflation, chaos, disorganization, confusion, misrepresentation, sensa-tionalism, disappearances, mysteries, illicit undertakings, drowning, asphyxiation, hospitals and charitable institutions, socialism, the theatre, glamour, sophistication, idealism, refinement, self-deception, deceit, fraud, disguises, intrigue, hoaxes, debauchery, seduction, day-dreaming, dreams, coma, hallucinations, vagueness, fog and cloud, camouflage, nebu-lousness, asylums, neuroses and madness, prisons, sanatoriums, obsession, rarefaction, poison, enchantment, perversion, scandal, slander, plots, seditions, synthetic materials, religious devotion and conversion, the highest forms of "spiritual" experience.

Practical interpretation

We look especially to Neptune in the birth-chart for the key to *necessary* sensitivity and potential subtlety and fineness of feeling, taste, or thought. This is the function within the psyche through which man may develop a sensitiveness that can con-tribute to his experiencing rare moments of inspiration, and through which he will feel the need to elevate himself in thought and behaviour—what some might term "spiritual upliftment". Neptune symbolizes the archetype of perfection.

A prominent Neptune will invariably—and one might sug-gest, *inevitably*—be found in the birth-charts (and hence denote a prominent Neptune-function in the make-up) of poets, artists, musicians and composers, and individuals whose humanitarian or social or practical religious work is expressed as an act of heart-felt dedication for the sole benefit of others. Neptune does not symbolize the Saturnian dutiful type of dedication that may, with all due respect, be a compulsive force for successful, ambitious achievements in the case of military leaders, politicians, or creed-bound sectarians. The archetypes correlated with the Neptunian psychic responses in man, tend to compel the individual to dissolve all forms or conditions of conformity, or man-made regulations which inhibit or restrict his natural path to self-realization.

The Neptunian type of sensitivity can only be creative and usefully applied if the individual is allowed freedom to recognize and to develop his own unique potential through this function. The Neptunian-sensitive person, by the very act of desiring and yielding to the subtle feelings and energies released through the archetypes responsible, becomes increasingly and perilously vulnerable to mental, emotional and nervous afflictions. His sensitivity exposes him to environmental pressures and conflicts that can precipitate disorganization, chaos, confusion, and abnormal states of anxiety and neuroses. It is no exaggeration when it is said that the division between genius and madness is a fearfully narrow and fragile boundary; and genius and madness are typical manifestations of archetypal activity symbolized by Neptune.

Looking to our example case presented in the chart on page 65, we find Neptune prominent because of its close ♂ MC, □ ☿, ✳☉, ♃♄. Potential artistic/creative ability has been realized by the subject, but the urge for *perfection* and subtlety of creative expression is felt to be best directed through *mental* channels of communication (Ψ □ rising ☿, ✳☉ in ♎) which is largely in the form of correspondence and authorship in his work. The subject's first thirty years were rather a classic example of Ψ ♂ MC—his difficulty in adjusting himself to a conventional career, as well as his utter lack of interest to do so. This was mainly because of a deep revulsion at the prospect of conforming to a stereotyped existence and an equally deep-felt desire to realize an ideal type of work in which he would not lose his identity as an individual and would retain relative freedom and independence. To some extent he has achieved his ideal, though not without corresponding mental and emotional strain ($\Psi \square \; \Beta m_{\downarrow}$) and experiencing periods of undermined health through the worry and stress of building an unorthodox business within the structure of a society that offered no scope or encouragement itself.

Esoteric astrologers proclaim the "sacred" and "divine" nature and purpose of the planet Neptune. It is "mystical consciousness or that innate sensitivity which leads unerringly to the higher vision".[1] Its keywords are "Divinity; Spirituality; Renunciation of self".[2] Max Heindel states that Neptune "carries what occultists know as the Father fire, the light and life of the Divine Spirit, which expresses itself as will".[3] My own thought-processes cannot interpret man and his psychological make-up in such mystical and nebulous language. Perhaps some readers may consider the theory of "archetypes" to be equally nebulous! What is, however, a very real thing, and which can be confirmed by any discriminating astrological student from the study of charts where the appropriate case-histories are known, is that Neptune symbolizes a sensitively impressionable, emotionally-charged part of man. Once aroused it will ever create an underlying restlessness, and fear of being confined and regulated. And yet, of course, it also represents that part of the psychic structure of man which can contribute most of all to his being ensnared in a self-woven net of confusion, instability and neurosis-producing intangible fears and anxieties.

Pluto (♇)

Primary function: Transformation.

Definition: To achieve a *transformation* in the organism through the elimination of a discordant or unwanted or tension-producing feature, and the formation of an entirely new feature.

Further definitions:

(a) A need to bring to the surface and into consciousness (from the *personal unconscious*) a discordant or inhibiting feature, an aggravating problem, a revealing truth, and possibly a root cause of a neurosis, that may have been long hidden or ignored and producing tensions and emotional disturbance. Such a content can no longer be contained by the organism in its existing form. It has to be completely *eliminated* or *transformed*.

(*b*) The function which suggests that the psyche as a whole may react drastically against a single feature which persists in disturbing its equilibrium, and seek to reject it from the system, or consciously transform the psychological content and accompanying energies into a new motive. Mostly this seems to be an involuntary process *forced upon* the individual by the gradual accumulation of discord and tension within, until, like a sudden volcanic or seismic eruption, the "festering" element must be released. The accompanying nervous-emotional reaction to the eruption is probably more the effects of the whole organism rebelling against this discordant feature than the effect of the feature itself as it is brought to light.

(*c*) The function that "corresponds to the *critical phase* in the cycle of life-force, or any process or activity, where death or the bringing to an end is inevitable, that rebirth or a new beginning can occur".[4]

(*d*) The function that *purges* in terms of psychological contents and nervous-emotional energies; the inborn safety-valve for the release of tensions and pent-up feelings and emotional energy.

(*e*) The function that may be seen as the means to "uncovering the skeleton in the cupboard", or shocking us with a glimpse of "the ghost from our past".

Contributes largely to:

(*a*) The development and fulfilment of the *self*, in terms of the necessary exposing and transforming of incohesive and discordant elements which oppose the process of integration of the self.

(*b*) The *personal unconscious*, in the sense that this Pluto-function is a natural process or outlet for the exposure of repressed and submerged contents of the personal unconscious.

(c) The *shadow*, as with regard to the personal unconscious.

Characteristic desire trends activated:

(a) A dramatic and usually drastic decision *to enforce a crisis* that must inevitably bring to an end or completely relieve a psychological complex, by the elimination of the environmental factors which created and maintained the complex.

(b) An *attitude of inevitability*, with accompanying determination not to be swayed from the course of action.

(c) A powerful awareness to the need for some form of *inner "regeneration"*; perhaps religious conversion, or a confession of guilt for something committed a long time ago.

(d) It is possible that on the *collective level* there can be a synchronized reaction among large numbers of individuals (perhaps under the persuasive influence and propaganda of a fanatical leader) to passionately enforce the elimination of an antagonistic or hated element, manifesting as mass hysteria, political blood-purges, mob lynchings. The increasing epidemic of world-wide student, political and industrial mass demonstrations and unrest of the "common peoples" during the 1960's and on into the 1970's was forecast by the present writer as a likely manifestation of the transits of Pluto and Uranus through Virgo.

(e) *Resistance to this eliminative function* within the psyche and continued suppression of the unpleasant and aggravating element that needs to be consciously faced up to, may be a cause of consequent obsessional and neurotic conditions, and in severe cases, probable eruptive outbursts of violent and self-destructive behaviour, and psychopathic conditions.

Traditional association with: The underworld of crime, mob violence, war, sex crimes, racketeering, gangsterism, mob lynchings, blood-purges, terrorist activities; abysses, sewers, drains, mines; transformation, transmutation, transfiguration, transition, translation, renewal, rejuvenation, resurrection, regeneration, the ending of a chapter of experience and the beginning of a new chapter; not the production of a fresh development of existing movements but a totally new departure; cataclysms, volcanic and seismic eruptions, atomic energy, cauterizing, subterranean activities, fumigation; collectiveness, group activity, multi-millionaires, "big-ness", colossal enter-prises; dictatorship; religious conversion; psycho-analysis; the sexual act, birth, and death—the crises of transformation processes in the cycle of life-energy; the "orgasm" of the sexual act—that eruption of the senses with the release of pent-up feelings and tension and excitement in their transformation to a new dimension of experience.

Practical interpretation

For many astrologers Pluto still remains very much of an enigma, and when this is the case, and one is unsure of one's interpretation of this chart factor, it is best left alone. Guess-work, or deceiving oneself into thinking that "intuition" will arrive at the correct answers, is not genuine astrology.

An interesting fact about Pluto is, however, that it represents elements in a man's life which for the larger period of their normally slow, submerged process of development, are more of an enigma than a reality of the kind that one can recognize and understand. The effects caused by these undercurrent pro-cesses, which mainly arise out of the personal unconscious, are either mostly ignored by the conscious mind or are registered as some sort of "psychic indigestion" that will presumably disappear if not dwelt upon.

But this Pluto-function within the psyche of man is relentless in its process of purging from the organism—psychic and otherwise—a discordant content. Nothing, absolutely nothing, can prevent it from executing its task of elimination and renewal. But let us be perfectly clear about this process, which can and does occur in the lives of every human being. It is not something that *just happens* without cause or justification. Initially there must be a happening which causes the Pluto-process to react and so be set "into motion". The initial actuating factor is always a *condition* that is created by the interaction of the individual with his environment. The con-dition has usually developed as the result of a series of dis-agreeable experiences associated with someone or some thing. There is a build up of tension, annoyance, frustration. Perhaps, in the majority of such instances, the conflict is suitably resolved, or the source of conflict removed without need for drastic action. But in certain cases it seems that intervention by the Pluto-function is the only means the psyche has left to rid itself of the discordant and upsetting condition. The function appears to operate initially without conscious command.

Actual events, which are a manifestation of the symbolic Plutonian "bringing to the surface" and into consciousness of the root cause of a discordant condition that needs to be got rid of, can synchronize with significant progressed and transiting aspects. Usually, by the time the Pluto-process has reached this external stage of eruption and exposure, the only and inevitable outcome is the "ending of a chapter of experience and the start of an entirely new chapter". A typical instance can be shown in the life of the subject of our example chart on page 65. His marriage had broken down on several previous occasions, and each time he and his wife "patched it up". But when during the same period Pluto by transit approached □ his ☽, and □ his wife's ♀; his wife's progressed ☉ came to exact ☌ her progressed ♇; his wife's progressed ☽ came to exact ☌ her ♇ and her progressed ☉ . . . the marriage finally and irretrievably broke down and they separated.

It would also seem that the psychic function symbolized by Pluto could be closely associated with *complexes* and with the psyche's attempts to free the individual from their influence. A peculiarity of the psychic structure is the tendency of ideas to become associated round certain basic nuclei, and Jung originated the term *complex* to describe these associated ideas.

A complex may be conscious (we are aware of it), or partly conscious, or totally unconscious. But what is known to be a very important feature is that complexes "are psychic contents which are *outside the control of* the conscious mind. They have been split off from consciousness, and lead a separate existence in the unconscious, being at all times ready to hinder or to reinforce the conscious intentions."[5] Complexes are "skeletons in the cupboard". They are "*vulnerable points* which we do not like to remember and still less to be reminded of by others, but which frequently come back to mind unbidden and in the most unwelcome fashion. They always contain memories, wishes, fears, duties, needs, or views, with which we have never really come to terms, and for this reason they constantly interfere with our conscious life in a disturbing and usually a harmful way."[6]

The *whole* birth-chart, and not simply Pluto, would need to be carefully studied for an assessment to be made of the potential *vulnerable* or weakest points (in the psyche) which could indicate the nature of significant complexes, and the most probable types of experience and environmental conflict from which complexes could originate. Jung has stressed that these vulnerable points or complexes are focal or nodal points of psychic life which we would not wish to do without. Complexes imply "that something incompatible, unassimilated, and conflicting exists—perhaps as an obstacle, but also as a stimulus to greater effort, and so, perhaps, as an opening to new possibilities of achievement".[7]

From my own personal study and experience of Pluto in countless charts I would suggest that we must look to Pluto by sign-placing and aspects for an indication of the most likely *attitude* the individual will by nature adopt towards complexes, or towards any other inner conflict or discord, as a means to aiding (consciously or unconsciously) the Pluto-process of elimination and transformation. Pluto's relation to the chart as a whole, but especially to particular planets it aspects, should also indicate other modes of psychic behaviour which could hinder or complicate the Plutonian process of transformation, or possibly strengthen its chances of successfully fulfilling its purpose.

NOTES

1. *Esoteric Astrology*, by Alice Bailey, p. 306 (Lucis Press Ltd., London).
2. *Transcendental Astrology*, by A. G. S. Norris, p. 241 (Rider & Co. London).
3. *The Message of the Stars*, p. 344 (L. N. Fowler & Co., Ltd., London).
4. *Teach Yourself Astrology*, by Jeff Mayo, p. 44 (The English Universities Press Ltd, London, 1964).
5. *Modern Man in Search of a Soul*, by Carl Jung, p. 90 (Kegan Paul, Trench, Trubner & Co. Ltd., 1944).
6. *Ibid.*, p. 91.
7. *Ibid.*, p. 91.

9 *Physiological and Anatomical Associations*

Physiology is the science of vital processes and bodily functions of living organisms. *Anatomy* is the study of the shape and structure of the various parts of the body. Some features of the human body have for many centuries been associated astrologically with the Sun or Moon or particular planets. It might be said with fair justification that successive generations of astrologers have tended to accept without question these traditional connections between the planets and the organs and functions of the physical body. And then, in defence of the astrologers, one could say that inevitably the vast majority who seriously study astrology must place their faith in traditional astro-anatomical correlations, because for various reasons each would individually be unable or could not devote adequate time to do the necessary statistical research to test the validity of these. It could also be said with equal justification based on the personal experience of individual astrologers, that the majority of these traditional astro-anatomical and astro-physiological correlations do seem to be valid.

For instance, the planet Mercury is traditionally associated with the respiratory system, and a strongly placed or afflicted Mercury in a birth-chart may be said to indicate respiratory troubles for the person concerned. Indeed, I personally would confirm that this is so, that an afflicted Mercury (in difficult aspect with other planets) can significantly indicate a respiratory system and also a nervous system vulnerable to health troubles. One cannot, however, be too adamant about such complaints, because the measure of health affliction is likely to be determined to a considerable extent by the nature of environmental conditions and stresses the person is subjected to. Also a carefully controlled and balanced diet, and avoidance of emotional and physical excesses, could help to prevent any noticeable manifestation of respiratory weaknesses or any significant nervous affliction. And yet the astrologer could be absolutely correct in stating that there is *potential* vulnerability to health troubles in connection with the respiratory system and through the nervous system generally. The essential implication here would be that this particular person would be *potentially prone to* this type of health trouble, in far greater measure than another person who has no astrological pointers to similar complaints.

Are we able to state exactly what is meant by the "association of a planet with a particular part of the human body"? This would be a very difficult question to answer with any degree of certainty, and at the present kindergarten stage of our understanding of astrology one's answer could only be theorizing. I would stress most strongly that the astrological student exercises the utmost caution when interpreting possible organic and physical troubles. Not only because the majority of students may have no medical training and qualifications, but because as yet insufficient research has been carried out to support or invalidate traditional astro-physiological theories. In speaking of a particular planet's "association with" a particular part of the body or a physiological function, we must not restrict ourselves to thinking that this planet alone, and no other planet, is so connected. What we should mean is that this particular planet has a far more significant connection with that physiological function or part of the body than has any of the other planets.

As to exactly how or why these planetary-physiological correlations exist—what can be the answer? It may be found that in most instances there is no *physical* connection in terms of cause and effect. And yet, we astrologers who are continually finding undeniable cases where a form of ill-health can be clearly diagnosed through the subject's birth-chart, would feel justified in believing that a physical process of cause and effect linking the cosmic bodies with the human body *must exist*.

What we can see is that in most instances the *nature* (in terms of its role within the organism) of a part of the human body, or of a particular physiological function, is related ideally with a planet whose *nature* (in terms of human psychological traits) has significant similarities. The fact that as yet we cannot explain why this is so would seem to be of less importance than the fact that astrologers are continually finding these correlations present in cases they examine. Now follows the physiological and anatomical correlations with each planet and the Sun and Moon. Indications are also given as regards the type of sickness and disease with which each cosmic body is especially connected. Traditional theories are included, whether the present author considers some of these to be valid or not. In compiling the lists of traditional theories very helpful reference was made to the massive volume, *Encyclopaedia of Medical Astrology*, written by the late Dr. Howard L. Cornell, M.D., LL.D.

The Sun (☉)

Physiological actions are: heat-generating, vitalizing, caloric-producing, integrating, combustive, dry, quickening, circulatory.

The heart and circulatory system. We all know that the heart is the most vital organ in the body. Its energizing, life-sustaining function clearly corresponds to the vital role and controlling influence of the Sun as the source of energy at the centre of its system of encircling planets. The heart governs and regulates the equilibrium of the whole body. Through the complex network of some 60,000 miles of tubing (the arteries, the veins, and the capillaries) blood is carried to all parts of the body by the energy that the heart's pumping action provides. Here we can see how the heart's controlling influence integrates every feature and each minute cell in the human organism. Through the arteries and veins warmth, vital energy, nutrients, oxygen, and the waste products of the body's metabolism are transmitted and distributed.

The thymus gland. I have long been inclined to believe that this endocrine gland is significantly associated with the Sun. It is thought that its most important function is during the formative childhood years, when it regulates the rhythms of growth and delays puberty until the required growth formation within the organism has been achieved. The thymus is also believed to be responsible for the immunological activity of the body against foreign antigens such as bacteria, and may be "intimately involved in the development of those reactions which make each one of us a *biologically unique individual*".[1]

Other traditional associations. The spleen. The back generally, though some have stressed the upper portion of the back, others the sides of the body. The right eye of males, the left eye of females. The brain generally. The right testicle.

Therapeutic properties of Sun remedies are: cardiac (affects the heart action); anticachectic (stimulating and tonic to prevent or improve any serious lowering of vitality and general bad state of health); sudorific (promoting perspiration); preservative (of good health and sound organs).

Typical traditionally associated therapeutic drugs. Aurum (gold); chamomilla; the sun-flower (helianthus); sinapis nigra and alba (mustard), both strong rubefacients.

Types of sickness and disease. Those directly concerning the heart, the blood, and the malfunctioning of the circulatory system and thymus gland. Anaemia, the leukaemias, Hodgkin's disease, the purpuras and haemophilia should all be closely investigated for probable correlation with an afflicted Sun.

Other physical afflictions traditionally observed. Organic, constitutional and structural diseases and defects. The Sun is most powerful in health matters when within 8° orb of conjunction an angle of the birth-chart. Chronic sickness. Acne. Apoplexy. Appendicitis. Biliousness. Organic brain defects. Carcinoma of the bowels or stomach. Catarrh. Diphtheria. Energy depletion. Fevers, inflammations and skin eruptions. Eye disorders and weak sight. Fainting and giddiness. Fistula. Haemorrhage. Hereditary diseases. Hyperaemia. Lameness or tumours in the knees. Weak legs. Measles. Migraine. Mouth disorders. Pimples. Polypus. Quinsy. Respiratory troubles. Scurvy. Pains in shoulders. Smallpox. Spinal disorders. Sunstroke. Swellings, especially in the neck, ankles and feet. Throat disorders. Venereal diseases.

The Moon (☽)

The Moon is certainly of equal importance to the Sun where the diagnosis of ill-health and malfunctioning of the human body is concerned. Its position in the birth-chart by sign, aspects with other planets, closeness to an angle, and if in the sixth or twelfth houses, can be important significators of a type of sickness. The Moon is said to regulate the course of an illness and to indicate the crisis period according to the Moon's transiting position relative to particular sensitive points in the birth-chart at the onset of the illness. This warrants careful research.

Physiological actions are: cold, moist, fertilizing, alterative, plastic, expulsive, cleansing, receptive, absorbent, convertive, metamorphic, secreting, periodic, mutational, fluidic, mediating.

The fluids and secreting functions. It is not only astrologers but also scientists who have confirmed the influence of the Moon upon water and fluids. Functional activities of the nature of and associated with the Moon indicate its connection with bodily fluids: fecundation, assimilation, secreting, dissolving processes. *Synovial fluid*, a lubricant secreted by certain membranes. *Perspiration* as a secretion, and the function of the sweat glands.

The lymphatic system. Lymph is a watery fluid which surrounds the majority of cells in the body and serves as a bridge across which nutriments, oxygen and wastes pass between the capillaries and the cells. The lymph has a special circulatory system of its own. It is from the lymph more so than from the blood that the tissues receive their nourishment and into it they excrete their waste products. The lymph filter through the body, aiding the process of digestion, draining excess tissue fluid, absorbing droplets of fat, and preventing infection from entering the bloodstream.

The digestive system. The digestive system begins at the mouth and ends at the anus. This system of course embraces a complex process involving the oesphagus, stomach, liver, pancreas and intestines. The Moon's principle association within this system is with the function and glands of the *stomach*, and the production of *gastric juices* and *chyle*; with *saliva* and the *salivary glands*; the *pancreatic juice*; the *intestinal juice* and secreting function of the numerous tiny glands in the small bowel; and *peristalsis*, the rhythmic alternate movements of contraction and relaxation by which the intestines and stomach propel their contents along.

The pancreas. This gland regulates sugar supplies for energy. It is noteworthy that low blood-sugar produces "emotional instability", a known symptom associated with the Moon. Its pancreatic juice is used in the digestion of food; it also produces insulin.

Female reproductive system. The menstrual cycle in the female organism provides one of the most challenging processes for research. Is it a coincidence that the length of the normal menstrual cycle is 28 days, approximately that of the Moon's mean sidereal period? There is no simple answer, short of thorough research, for menstruation is a complicated cycle controlled by the internal secretions of the ovary and of the pituitary. The entire female reproductive system must be considered closely associated with the Moon and its relationship to the whole birth-chart for an individual.

The breasts. These mammary glands are accessories of the reproductive system, designed for milk production in the female.

Sympathetic nervous system. The basis of this system is a chain of ganglia running the length of each side of the spinal column from one end to the other, and it is responsible for man's automatic and spontaneous reflexes which do not come under the influence of the will or his consciousness. It is connected with nutrition, elimination, and protection of the organism, and with emotions, affections and desires.

Other traditional associations. Oesophagus. Left eye of the male, right eye of the female. Cavities and receptacles of the body. Cellular tissue building. Cerebellum. Corpulency and fleshiness. Gall bladder (as a receptacle). Left side of the body. Osmosis (the percolation and intermixture of fluids separated by porous membrane). Pericardium (membrane around heart). The absorbent and lymphatic vessels of the respiratory system. Mucous and serous surfaces. The left testicle. The thoracic cavity. Thyroid gland. Tonsils. Uvula (pendent fleshy outgrowth at back of palate). Zymotic (fermentation) action. Normally represents a cleansing, alterative and expulsive influence.

Therapeutic properties of Moon remedies are: Alterative (medicinal effects which alter the processes of nutrition or excretion); attenuant (increasing the fluidity of the blood or other secretions by thinning these); emetic (causing vomiting). *Typical traditionally associated therapeutic drugs.* Agaricus, argentum, colocynth, pellitory.

Types of sickness and disease. Pancreatitis, cysts, adenomas, diabetes, and hypoglycaemia due to the Moon's connection with the pancreas. Digestive disorders. Synovitis. Irregular menses and general gynaecological complaints and abortions. *Other physical afflictions traditionally observed.* Abscesses. Diseases of alimentary canal. Anaemia. Aneurysm. Apoplexy. Asthma. Bladder disorders. Blood disorders. Boils. Breast disorders. Bronchitis. Carcinoma, especially of the stomach and breasts. Chlorosis. Cholic. Consumption. Convulsions. Delirium tremens. Diarrhoea. Dropsical swellings. Duodenal ulcers. Epilepsy. Eye disorders and blindness. Fainting. Flatulence. Genito-urinary disorders. Gout. Haemoglobin defects. Stones in kidneys. Lameness. Laryngitis. Lunacy. Measles. Diseases of the mucous and serous membranes. Nervous disorders of a highly-strung and hysterical type. Neuralgia. Paralysis. Pimples. Pleurisy. Poisoning of the system. Quinsy. Rheumatism. Ringworm. Scrofula. Scurvy. Shingles. Smallpox. Sore throats. Excessive sweating. Tumours. Ulcers. Varicose veins. Vomiting.

Mercury (☿)

Physiological actions are: nervine (acting on the nerves), periodic, exciting, activating, irregularity, cold, dry, restless, changeable, connective, co-ordinating, corrosive, debilitating, irritating, spasmodic.

Central nervous system. Mercury is primarily associated in life with all forms of *communication,* and this same principle is seen in the physiological functions with which this planet is significantly connected. The most typical Mercurian process is that of the basic behavioural pattern characteristic of all *nervous* organizations: excitation, conduction, integration. The entire body of man is covered by an intricate network of nerve fibres, and the central nervous system is the means by which all bodily activities are co-ordinated and by which man responds to changes in his environment. Functionally speaking, this nervous system can be divided into three parts: nervous structures which convey incoming impulses from the skin and sense organs, the central structure which is primarily that of the brain, and the nervous structures which conduct outgoing messages towards the periphery. Anatomically speaking, the central nervous system consists of the *brain*, the *spinal cord*, and the innumerable nerves to which these give rise. The principle of Mercury is clearly typified in the central nervous system which co-ordinates all nerve impulses and reflexes, and which serves conscious functions and has enabled man to develop his faculties of thinking and reasoning. Mercury must also be connected with the *sympathetic nervous system* which regulates the purely automatic functions of the body, such as the activity of the glands and the viscera, distinct from the central nervous system which is chiefly concerned with sensations and movements.

The sensory system. Strictly speaking the sensory organs are not usually classified as a separate bodily system, being vital features of the nervous system. However, through the nervous and sensory systems and the lungs man receives the impress of his environment, and Mercury's co-ordinating and communicating principles can be recognized in the functions of all the sense perceptions, as seeing, hearing, feeling, smelling, tasting.

Thyroid gland. Its secretion controls the rate of body metabolism and of combustion of air in breathing. Excess causes over-excitability and nervousness. Deficiency in childhood can cause cretinism, and in adulthood, an obese slow-wittedness.

Respiratory system. This includes the nose and naso-pharynx, the trachea or windpipe, the bronchi, and the lungs. Through the lungs oxygen is adapted for transmitting to all parts of the body, and carbon dioxide that has accumulated as a waste product in the body's tissues is conveyed by the venous blood to the capillaries of the lungs where the gas is exhaled.

Other traditional associations. Arms. Bowels. Ears. Feet. Gall bladder. Hair. Hands. Hips. Knees. Legs. Mouth. Shoulders. Sight. Tongue. Vocal cords.

Therapeutic properties of Mercury's remedies are: alterative (medicinal affects which alter the processes of nutrition or excretion); antiperiodic (destroying the periodicity of diseases that run a typical course); cephalic (relieving disorders of the head); cholagogue (purgative expelling bile); nervine (a nerve tonic, relieving nervous disorders).

Typical traditionally associated therapeutic drugs. Apiol, avena, calomel, Mercury, parsley, petroselinum, podophyllin.

Types of sickness and disease. Respiratory disorders. Sickness of nervous origin and neurological diseases. Mental afflictions. Thyroid disorders, particularly goitre.

Other physical afflictions traditionally observed. Apoplexy. Asthma. Back pains. Breathing troubles. Cholera. Colic. Consumption. Convulsions. Coughs. Cramps, especially in the limbs. Deafness. Delirium. Dizziness. Dumbness. Epilepsy. Eye disorders. Feet complaints. Flatulence. Gall bladder disorders. Gastro-abdominal disorders. Gonorrhoea. Gout. Hair troubles. Hay fever. Headaches. Hips—especially gout. Hyperaesthesia (hyper-sensitivity). Insanity. Insomnia. Lameness. Locomotor ataxia. Memory defects. Neuralgia. Neurasthenia. Nasal disorders. Paralysis. Phrenitis. Rheumatism. Spasmodic pains. Speech impediments. Worms.

Venus (♀)

Physiological actions are: centripetal, moist, warm, nourishing, conserving, fermenting, proliferation, congesting, emetic, enlarging, fertilizing, lethargic, non-malignant, pustular, relaxing, rhythmical, gradual.

Venous circulation. The system of *veins*, distinct from *arteries*, which in effect is a *centripetal* process. Blood is driven into the arteries from the heart and distributed to all parts of the body as the arteries divide into smaller branches and finally into a meshwork of microscopic vessels called capillaries. This meshwork joins up again to form small veins, which become large venous trunks through which blood is carried centrally towards the heart. Veins have no pulse.

Parathyroid glands. Four small structures embedded in the thyroid capsule, which regulate the metabolism of calcium and phosphorus, indispensable for the building of the skeleton which gives *form* and *holds together* the human organism. *Kidneys.* In my earlier years as an astrology student I had felt that Venus had merely been chosen to be connected with the kidneys because it is the planet ruling Libra (the sign traditionally associated with the kidneys). Even so, again and again I found Venus to be the most likely indicator of kidney trouble in charts. The fact that the kidneys' prime role seemed to be that of a pair of filters removing the waste products of metabolism from the blood did not correlate at all clearly with the Venus principle. Until I realized that the kidneys' essential activity is the maintenance of a *constant* composition of the circulating blood.

The throat and genital regions. These physical parts are associated with the Taurus (ruled by Venus)-Scorpio polarity. Venus is a factor associated with erotic desires and forms of emotional expression, and it is a fact that disorders of the genitals and reproductive system often has evident ill-effects for the throat, and vice versa.

Other traditional associations. Aural ducts. Breasts. Cellular tissue building. Cheeks. Chin. Eustachian tubes. Lips, especially upper lip. Lumbar region. Navel. Neck. Olfactory nerve (the nerve of smell). Ovaries. Semen and seminal vesicles. Skin of face. Stomach (veins of). Thymus gland. Uterus.

Therapeutic properties of Venus remedies are: antinephritic (for use against inflammation and diseases of the kidneys); diuretic (promoting the flow of urine); demulcent (soothing, allaying irritation); emetic (causing vomiting).

Typical traditionally associated therapeutic drugs. Copper (cuprum), pulsatilla.

Types of sickness and disease. Associated with the malfunctioning of the venous circulation; the parathyroids, such as tetany in extreme cases of calcium and phosphorus deficiency, and generalised osteitis fibrosa cystica in extreme cases of glandular secretion; the kidneys; the throat; the internal genito-urinary system.

Other physical afflictions traditionally observed. Atrophy. Bilious flatulency. Blackheads. Bladder diseases. Breast disorders. Bright's disease. Carcinoma. Cellular metamorphosis. Chilblains. Colds in the head. Consumption. Contagious diseases. Cysts. Debility. Diabetes. Diet indiscretions. Diphtheria. Dropsy. Dysentery. Epidemics. Epigastrium disorders. Eyes (discharges from). Feet (skin eruptions). Fistula. Gonorrhoea. Gout. Growths. Heartburn. Hernia. Impotency. Impure blood. Incontinence. Leucorrhoea. Lumbago. Measles. Neck swellings. Obesity. Poisoning. Pustular outbreaks and diseases. Ringworm. Rupture. Scrofula. Scurvy. Skin eruptions. Smallpox. Sores. Spinal disorders. Sterility. Swellings (glandular). Syphilis. Thorax disorders. Throat disorders. Tonsilitis. Tuberculosis. Tumours. Typhus fever. Ulceration. Uremia. Venereal diseases generally. Vomiting. Worms.

Mars (♂)

Physiological actions are: centrifugal, inflammatory, acute, forcing, destructive, hot, dry, combustive, disruptive, dynamic, energizing, exciting, expulsive.

The muscular system. This is the intricate machinery by which manipulation and activation of the skeleton and functional processes within the organism can be performed, and through which *power* is expressed. This is ideally associated with the principle of Mars.

Urogenital system and gonads (sex glands). The expulsive and centrifugal action of Mars is evident here: the waste fluids of the *bladder* being eliminated as urine through the outer orifice of the *genitals*; the ejection of sperm from the *male testes*; the shedding of eggs from the *female ovaries*. The Mars glyph significantly resembles the male *penis* in erection.

The adrenals. The principle of Mars within the physical body is one of the most important factors of attack and resistance against foreign bodies and disease. We see this in the natural processes of inflammations and fever. But it is particularly evident in the action of the adrenals which have been called the "fight and flight" glands of the endocrine system. Under stress of fear or anger its secretions pour into the bloodstream. This secretion we know as adrenaline can stimulate the heart, raise the blood-pressure, deepen the respiration, increase the blood-sugar which supplies fuel for the muscles, and prepare the body to fight or resist forces from without.

Sympathetic nervous system. This vast network of nerve

fibres functions as automatic response and as *emergency and protective activity*, mostly of an unconscious nature. It is the inborn, instinctive means by which the activity of the glands and viscera are regulated. It aids elimination processes, and is intimately linked with the source of emotions and desires situated at the rear of the brain.

Red blood cells. These cells outnumber the white cells 700 to 1. Their exclusive job is to transport oxygen from the lungs to the rest of the body and to convey waste carbon dioxide back the other way. They do this because of their content of haemoglobin, a compound of protein and *iron* which gives blood its red colour. A deficiency in haemoglobin results in anaemia. Although astrological textbooks have always given preference to red blood cells over white cells where connection with Mars is concerned, it may be that the white cells have equal right to be associated with Mars. They constitute the blood's "mobile guard", rallying in vast numbers to engulf and destroy invading bacteria anywhere in the body.

The kidneys. Hormone secretions from the adrenals control the kidneys' function, which is excretory and not just a filter activity for waste matter.

Other traditional associations. Bile, Blood fibrin. Cerebral ganglia. Cerebral hemisphere (left). Ear (left). Fibrous tissue building. Gall and gall bladder. Head generally. Motor nerves. Motor segment of spinal cord. Naso-pharynx. Nose. Rectum. Sinews. Smell (sense of). Sthenic process (abnormally active) in the body. Taste (sense of). Vaso-dilator action of the cerebral ganglia.

Therapeutic properties of Mars remedies are: aphrodisiac (stimulating sexual desire); caustic; resolvent (removing swelling or effusion; relieving rheumatic pains); rubefacient (counter-irritant); stimulating; vesicant (for raising blisters on the skin).

Typical traditionally associated therapeutic drugs. Arnica, arsenic, bryonia, cantharides (used as a rubefacient and for blistering; principle drug for increasing sexual desire), capsicum (red pepper, used in strong pain liniments), iron, nux vomica, quinine (the bitter alkaloid found in bark of cinchona, its sulphate used as febrifuge to allay fever, and as a tonic), sarsaparilla, strychnine, sulphur.

Types of sickness and disease. Associated with the malfunctioning of the muscular system; the genito-urinary system; the adrenals; the sympathetic nervous system; the blood; and the kidneys (such as stones, nephritis, pyelitis).

Other physical afflictions traditionally observed. The fevers and inflammations associated with Mars are typically quick developing, destructive, and often contagious. Abortion. Abrasions. Accidents. Aneurysm (localized bulging in the wall of an artery). Angina. Ankylosis. Bladder disorders. Bleeding. Blindness (especially through accident or smallpox). Blisters. Blood vessels (rupture of). Boils. Bowel inflammations. Brain fever. Bruising. Calculi (stones in bladder). Carbuncles. Cerebro-spinal disorders. Chickenpox. Cholera. Conjunctivitis. Consumption. Contagious fevers. Cutaneous (skin) eruptions. Cuts. Diabetes. Diarrhoea. Diphtheria. Dysentery. Dysuria. Enteric fever. Epidemics. Epilepsy. Erysipelas. Fatty degeneration of the heart. Fistula. Fractures. Gonorrhoea. Gravel. Haemoptysis (spitting up of blood from the chest). Haemorrhages. Haemorrhoids. Hernia. Herpes. High blood pressure. Hydrophobia (rabies). Hyperaemia (the congestion of a part with blood). Hypertrophy. Hysteria. Infections. Insanity. Jaundice. Left ear afflictions. Liver disorders. Malaria. Malignant diseases. Mania. Measles. Metorrhagia. Migraine. Nasal disorders. Nerve inflammations. Palpitations. Pneumonia. Poisoning. Puerperal fever. Quinsy. Rectum disorders. Rheumatism. Ringworm. Rupture. Scabies. Scalds. Scarlet fever. Sciatica. Scrofula. Shingles. Skin eruptions. Smallpox. Sores. Spinal diseases. Stomach inflammations. Sunstroke. Sweats (excessive). Swellings. Syphilis. Tonsilitis. Typhoid fever. Ulcers. Urethritis. Vagina ulcerations. Venereal diseases generally. Worms.

Jupiter (♃)

Physiological actions are: healing, harmonizing, preservation, restoration, conservation of energies, growth and expansion, aiding assimilation, filtration, heat production and temperance, nourishing, recuperation, phagocytosis (devouring process of invading germs by special cells amongst the white corpuscles of the blood, and the process of repairing injured tissue).

The liver. This is the largest gland in the body, and it seems apt that the largest planet in our Solar System should therefore be traditionally connected with it. I doubt whether that was the original reason for man linking the two together astrologically. An important function of the liver is the production of bile, which is a means of getting rid of waste, and is also an aid to the digestion, especially of *fats*. Any interference with the flow of bile tends to produce indigestion and flatulence in the bowels. It is interesting that astrologers always look to Jupiter in a chart for any indications of a tendency for putting on weight. Other functions of the liver are the neutralization of poisons (e.g. drugs, alcohol, bacterial toxins), production and storage of energy-producing glucose in the form of glycogen, formation of urea and uric acid, and it also operates like a huge sponge and can store a large amount of blood which it pours out when there has been loss of blood or retains when there is risk of over-distension of the heart by too much blood. We can see here the principle of Jupiter, to harmonize, preserve, restore and act as the regulator of uniform growth.

Posterior lobe of the pituitary gland. It was Rodney Collin who first suggested Jupiter's association with the posterior lobe of the pituitary gland, and Saturn's connection with the anterior lobe.[2] Astrologically, the Sun, Jupiter and Saturn are the prime factors in regard to *growth* in the human organism. The Sun generates and sustains growth, and gives the growing entity its unique identity; Jupiter represents the means for expansion, and that which regulates uniformity of growth, and compensates for inadequacies within the organism, corrects, restores, accumulates; whilst Saturn represents those processes that give form, solidity, and structural limits in terms of its control over the growing organism. The function of the anterior lobe is described under Saturn in this chapter. The posterior lobe helps to regulate the water-balance of the body, increases the tone of involuntary muscle generally, and would seem to provide a healing and harmonizing function.

Other traditional associations. Adipose tissue. Adrenals. Amniotic fluid. Arms. Arteries. Auricle (right) of heart.

Carbohydrates. Cell development, division, reproduction, and cellular tissue building. Digestive organs and functions. Feet. Fibrin of blood. Haematopoiesis (blood making). Hands. Hydrocarbonates (heat-giving foodstuff, e.g. sugars, starches, cellulose). Lungs. Phagocytes (special cells which devour invading germs and bacteria). Pleura. Ribs. Right ear. Semen. Sides of the body. Suprarenal capsules. Teeth. Thighs.

Therapeutic properties of Jupiter remedies are: alexipharmic (acting as antidote against poison); analeptic (restorative); anthelmintic (a remedy expelling intestinal worms); antispasmodic (for use against muscular spasms); balsamic (soothing, healing, of the nature of balsam); emollient (softens and relaxes the tissues to which applied).

Typical traditionally associated therapeutic drugs. Eupatorium, ginseng, iridin (iris), peppermint (mentha), stannum.

Types of sickness and disease. Associated with the malfunctioning of the liver and the posterior lobe of the pituitary gland. Arising through indiscretions and excesses in eating and drinking.

Other physical afflictions traditionally observed. Abscesses. Adipose sarcoma. Albumen, waste of, and excess of in the urine. Aneurysm. Apoplexy. Arterial blood disorders. Back disorders. Biliousness. Bladder (stone or abscess in). Blood poisoning. Boils. Breast carcinoma. Bronchitis. Calculus. Carbuncles. Carcinoma generally. Carotid arteries (fullness of). Cellular inflammation. Cerebral congestion. Choleric distemper. Colic. Congestions. Consumption. Corpulence. Cramps. Cysts. Dental decay. Diabetes Mellitus. Digestive disorders. Dropsy. Eczema. Epidemics. Epistaxis. Faintings. Fatty degeneration. Feet (cysts in). Festerings. Flatulence. Fluid accumulations. Haemorrhoids. Heart (enlarged; fatty degeneration). High blood pressure. Indigestion. Inflammation of the lungs. Jaundice. Kidney disorders. Knees (swellings in). Lardaceous carcinoma. Lumbago. Lung congestion. Moles. Pleurisy. Pneumonia. Poisoning. Quinsy. Sarcoma. Scrofula. Scurvy. Swellings. Toxaemia. Tumours. Vomiting. Warts.

Saturn (♄)

Physiological actions are: binding, cooling, crystallizing, hardening, depleting, obstructing, limiting, retarding, suppressing, centripetal, clotting, coagulating, contracting, condensing, constricting, defensive, consolidating, emaciating, granulating, retentive.

The skeletal system. In the physical body Saturn ideally corresponds to the functions of bone which are the provision of a framework to support the body and as a basis for form, the protection of internal organs, and as points of attachment for muscles.

The skin. The skin functions as a protective and as a sensory agent, and it also plays an essential role in the regulation of body temperature. We can see the principle of Saturn corresponding not to the protective aspect so much, as to the skin representing a necessary boundary, structural limit.

Anterior lobe of pituitary gland. The pituitary gland is only the size of a large pea, and yet it is the most important of all the endocrine glands. Because of the control it exercises over the other glands it has been called the "conductor of the endocrine orchestra". This particularly applies to the anterior lobe that has a great variety of functions concerned with fundamental aspects of body-build and character, structural formation of bones and muscles, promotion of masculine traits, regulation of the sex glands. Underdevelopment of this lobe produces dwarfism, whilst increased activity leads to gigantism.

Other traditional associations. Ears (especially right ear). Calcium deposits. Calves of legs. Cartilage. Cartilaginous tissue. Catabolism changes. Cervical vertebrae. Chyle. Circulation of the blood in the tissues. Cutaneous capillary vasocontrictor nerves. Endocardium. Faeces. Gall bladder. Gristle. Leukocytes. Ligaments. Lime deposits. Liver. The peripheral sympathetic nerves. Pneumogastric or vagus nerve. Sigmoid flexure. Spleen. Teeth. Tendons. Urea. Uric acid.

Therapeutic properties of Saturn remedies are: antiphlogistic (counteracting inflammation); antipyretic (fever-reducing); astringent (binding; tending to contract organic tissue and stop discharges); diuretic (promoting the flow of urine); febrifuge (lessens fever); refrigerant (cooling; reducing inflammation or fever); sedative; styptic (checks haemorrhage).

Typical traditionally associated therapeutic drugs. Aconite, antimony, astringents, belladonna, conium (hemlock), helleborus, hyoscyamus, hydrocyanic acid, Indian hemp, lead, mullein, rhus toxicodendron, salicylate of soda, tincture saturnina.

Types of sickness and disease. Associated with the skeletal system and including tendency to fractures and dislocations. Bone deformities, club foot; skin irritations and diseases, such as cutis, cyanosis, eczema, herpes, psoriasis; teeth decay, pyorrhoea; pituitary gland malfunctions; gall bladder afflictions, stones; spleen malfunctioning.

Other physical afflictions traditionally observed. Abortion. Adynamia. Ague. Antiperistalsis. Apoplexies. Arm infirmities. Arterio-sclerosis. Arthritis. Articular rheumatism. Asphyxia. Asthma. Ataxia. Atrophy, Auricular disease. Barrenness. Black jaundice. Blemishes. Blindness. Bright's Disease. Bunions. Calculus. Carcinoma generally. Caries. Cataract. Catarrh. Chilblains, Chills, Cirrhosis. Claw hand. Cloaca. Clots (blood). Colic. Constipation. Consumption. Corns. Cramps. Deafness. Diarrhoea. Dropsy. Dysmenorrhea. Dyspepsia. Dyspnoea. Emaciation. Embolism. Endocarditis. Enteralgia. Enteric fever. Epilepsy. Erysipelas. Fainting. Fetid conditions. Fibrous tumours. Fistula. Gastric disorders. Glaucoma. Goitre. Gout. Gravel. Haematoma. Hair disorders. Hemiplegia. Haemorrhoids. Hernia. Impediments. Impotency. Lameness. Leprosy. Leucorrhea. Lithemia. Lock jaw. Locomotor ataxia. Lumbago. Marasmus. Mastoid abscess. Menses (disorders of and irregularities). Mental disorders (especially of a depressive type). Micturition disorders. Moles. Mumps. Mydriasis. Myopia. Neuralgia. Oesophagus disorders. Palsy. Paraesthesia. Paralysis. Parotid gland disorders. Pectoral affections. Phthisis. Pimples. Pneumonia. Prolapsus. Prostatic stricture. Pulmonary diseases. Pyrosis. Rectum disorders. Rheumatism. Rickets. Rupture. Sciatica. Sclerosis. Scrofula. Stammering. Strangulations. Strangury. Strictures. Subluxations. Sweat process disorders. Thrombosis. Thyroid gland disorders. Tonsilitis. Toxaemia. Tuberculosis. Tumours. Typhus fever. Ulcers. Uremia. Urethra (stricture of). Urinary disorders. Varicose veins. Venereal diseases.

Uranus (♅)

Physiological actions are: neuralgic, exciting, disrupting, separating, convulsive, cramping, distorting, erratic, freak-producing, inco-ordinating, irregular, lesional, rupturing, shock-producing, spasmodic, straining, strictural, tension-producing, vibratory, lacerating.

Sympathetic nervous system. A description of this system has been given under the headings for the Moon, Mercury and Mars. Disease and disorders associated with Uranus are of primarily nervous origin, with symptoms of a dramatic, highly excitable, unusual, or spasmodic nature. A significant correlation with the sympathetic nervous system is likely. Affects are known to aggravate mental disorders of an excitable and convulsive type, and to result in nervous breakdowns, hysteria, extreme palpitation. At the "change of life" for both sexes the sympathetic nervous system seems to be more *unstable* than is normal, which is interesting in view of the fact that transiting Uranus opposes its own position in the natal chart (of each one of us) around this period in life.

Pineal body. This gland seems likely to be closely connected with the function of Uranus in man. It is the size of a small pea and projects from the roof and hind part of the brain. Though modern physiologists attach little importance to its role within the endocrine system, tumours in this gland have been observed to produce accelerated sexual development and great mental precocity. By some it is thought to be a relic of a third eye, which occultists associate with spiritual vision and psychic clairvoyance when this gland is activated by special mental exercises.

Gonads or sex glands. There is ample evidence that a strongly placed Uranus in a chart can be found in cases of sexual perversion, which supports the belief that this planet is a significant indicator of disorders or abnormal activity of sex gland secretions.

Other traditional associations. Ankles. Appendix. Brain (membranes of). Eyes. Nerve fluids. Heart valves. Kidneys (circulation in). Motor nerves of speech. Pituitary body. Respiratory action. Spinal cord membranes. Stomach membranes.

Therapeutic properties of Uranus remedies. Not known by the author.

Typical traditionally associated therapeutic drugs. Croton oil, ether, compressed air and gases.

Types of sickness and disease. Of nervous origin chiefly; aggravated by mental activity of an hysterical and highly-strung nature; pineal body malfunctioning; genital disorders, including venereal diseases.

Other physical afflictions traditionally observed. Accidents, especially through electricity, machinery, lightning. Appendicitis. Asthma. Bowel cramps. Brain disorders and peculiarities. Breathing (irregular). Claustrophobia. Colic. Contortions. Cramps. Emphysema. Eye afflictions. Fits. Floating kidney. Abnormal or freak growth. Heart palpitations and irregular beating. Hiccough. Insanity. Lesions. Motor nerve disturbances. Neuralgia. Numbness. Opisthotonos. Paralysis. Paroxysms generally. Pituitary body disorders. Prolapsus. Respiratory disorders of nervous origin. Rupture. Saint Vitus Dance. Speech impediment. Strictures. Torticollis. Urethra (spasm and stricture of). Valvular diseases of the heart.

Neptune (Ψ)

Physiological actions are: dispersive, refining, comatic, relaxing.

Spinal canal; spinal cord. The theory that Neptune is significantly connected with the spinal cord and canal possibly originated through Neptune's association with fluids, and because persons in whom the Neptune factor is prominent tend to have a highly sensitive mental, nervous and sensory reaction to exterior stimuli and to environmental conditions. The network of nerves which thread the body is rooted both in the spinal cord and the brain. Certainly the nervous and mental processes generally can be connected with the Neptune function in man.

Thalamus. Neptune is especially associated with the *emotions.* Modern research has shown that the thalamus, lying at the base of the brain, is intimately linked with man's emotional life. The disturbed and strained condition we know as *anxiety* is a Neptunian type of condition, and it is interesting that in the operation of leucotomy the fibres connecting the frontal areas of the cerebral hemispheres (which play an important part in determining our patterns of behaviour) with the thalamus are severed. The purpose of this operation is to remove the intense anxiety which is associated with many forms of insanity.

Other traditional associations. Amoeboid cellular activity. Appendix. Cellular reproduction and tissue-building. Cerebral ventricles. Conjunctiva. Cytoplaslema. Eyes. Glands (of legs, arms, hands, feet, stomach, genito-urinary system). Insanity. Nerve fibres. Optic nerve. Pineal gland.

Therapeutic properties of Neptune remedies are: analgesic (alleviates pain); anodyne (alleviates pain); hallucinating; relaxing; sedative; soporific (sleep-inducing).

Typical traditionally associated therapeutic drugs. Narcotics such as cocaine, morphine, heroin, opiates, and other soporifics and stimulants; anodyne; chloroform, ether, iodine.

Types of sickness and disease. Chiefly of nervous and emotional origin, which probably explains why "mysterious" pains and sickness—because their origin cannot be traced— are invariably experienced by persons with a prominent Neptune in their birth-chart. Afflictions to the thalamus, spinal cord, nervous system and mental processes. Alcoholism and drug-addiction. Affliction or death by gassing, drowning, poisoning.

Other physical afflictions traditionally observed. Amoebic dysentery. Anaemia. Appendicitis. Atrophy. Blindness. Brain disorders. Carcinomas. Catalepsy. Catalysis. Claustrophobia. Consumption. Debility, as a result of fears, phobias, anxiety, neurotic states of mind. Deformities. Dropsy. Eye troubles, especially conjunctivitis, myopia, nyctalopia. Fainting. Feet (wasting of tissues). Fingers (horny nails on). Fluid disorders. Glands (swelling and wasting). Infantile paralysis. Influenza. Necrosis. Pyorrhoea. Saint Vitus Dance. Septic poisonings. Venereal diseases.

Pluto (♇)

I would make a tentative suggestion that the Pluto function in the physiological sense is with the creative and regenerative forces. There may be a significant connection with the sexual organs. Astrologers have assigned Pluto to rulership of the zodiacal sign Scorpio, which also is associated with the sexual organs. We may find Pluto prominent in cases of deep-rooted diseases that take a very long time making themselves evident and "coming to the surface". From my own experience of studying charts of obsessional cases I have invariably found Pluto strongly placed and afflicted. I would think, too, that when extensive research has been undertaken in regard to carcinomas, we may well find a strongly afflicted Pluto or an angular Pluto present in most cases of incurable carcinoma. Eliminative and purging processes of the human organism should be borne in mind. One would also think of skin eruptions and boils as a Plutonian function, the throwing out of poisonous and unwanted matter.

NOTES

1. Editorial, *The British Medical Journal*, 29 September 1962.
2. *The Theory of Celestial Influence*, by Rodney Collin (Vincent Stuart London).

10 *The Psychic Structure of Man*

I have felt it necessary to devote this chapter to a brief explanation of several of the Jungian concepts of the psychic structure of man, as most of these will be referred to in connection with the planets' correlation with potential human behaviour. The two diagrams (figs. 2 and 3), though very inadequate, may help

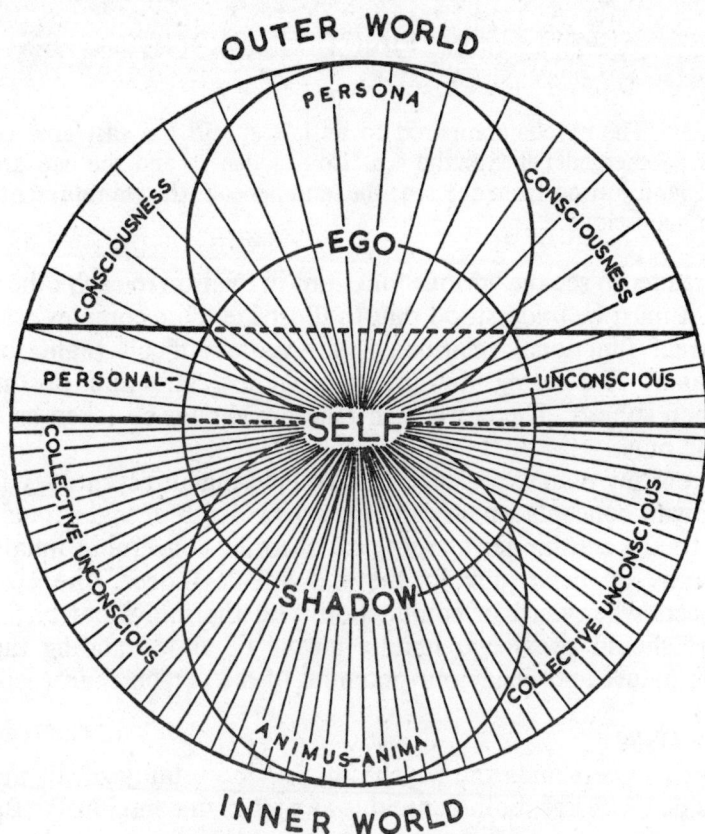

Fig. 2. The Totality of the Psyche.[1]

[1] After a diagram in *The Psychology of Jung*, by Jolan Jacobi, p. 121 (Routledge & Kegan Paul Ltd, 1942).

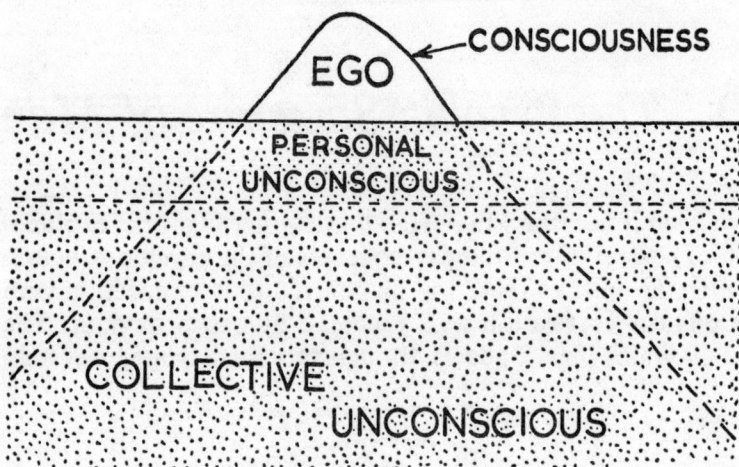

Fig. 3. The psyche compared to an island and the vast area of land submerged beneath the sea. Consciousness and the ego are the island jutting from the sea; the land beneath the sea represents the unconscious.

the reader to see the various functions in relation to each other. But it must be understood that to illustrate these complex and abstract functional relations is far more difficult than, for instance, illustrating the internal *physical* structure of the human subject. Therefore each diagram should be taken as a guide only.

From my own experience I find that Jungian psychology is rich with concepts which can give a new depth of understanding to the traditional astrological theories concerning innate patterns of behaviour in the individual. Indeed, the two subjects when used in conjunction with the individual birth-chart should provide a unique means of understanding the basic nature and behaviour potential of the person concerned.

The Psyche

Jung understands the psyche to be "the totality of all the psychic processes, both conscious as well as unconscious".[1] By the concept of *totality* Jung means more than unity or wholeness. "It implies a kind of integration, a unification of parts, a a creative synthesis that includes some active power of the psyche. It is an entity, concomitant to the concept of the 'self-regulating system'."[2] Thus, in Fig. 2 the psyche is represented by the outer circle, embracing both consciousness and the unconscious aspects of the individual.

The terms *psyche* and *psychic* are not to be confused with similar terms used by occultists and spiritualists to describe supernormal phenomena, extra sensory perception, or as a term for a spiritualist medium or sensitive. Jung chose these terms so as to avoid the confusion that can arise from the everyday use of the terms *mind* and *mental* activity. In the Jungian system *mind* and *mental* activity are associated primarily with *conscious* psychological activity, and this will be their meaning within this book.

It is important to remember that the psyche embraces both consciousness and the unconscious. The idea of the psyche has often been compared to an island (Fig. 3) and the vast, boundless expanse of land it is a part of: the island is the very small portion that is visible above the water, and this is consciousness and the *ego*, whilst the greater portion that is below the water represents the dark, unknown realm of the unconscious.

The psyche is not a static thing, it is a *dynamic* system, in constant movement, regulated by its own laws. Everything made by man had its beginnings in the psyche. Everything man experiences, pain, desire, changing moods, is psychic.

Astrologically, the psyche is represented by the whole chart-pattern—planets, signs, aspects, and the angles of the chart.

Libido or Psychic Energy

The general psychic energy is called *libido*. The Freudian use of this word is entirely sexual. But Jung speaks of libido as psychic energy which is capable of as many transformations and interchanges as is physical energy. Libido is the creative principle of life, animating all conscious expression. This energy does not imply a *force*, any more than does the concept of energy in physics. Actually it is defined as the *intensity* of the psychic process, its *psychological value*, which is determined only through its psychological manifestations and effects.

The Collective Unconscious; Personal Unconscious

The unconscious is in two parts: the *personal* unconscious and the *collective* unconscious. "The collective unconscious is a part of the psyche which can be negatively distinguished from a personal unconscious by the fact that it does not, like the latter, owe its existence to personal experience and consequently is not a personal acquisition. While the personal unconscious is made up essentially of contents which have at one time been conscious but which have disappeared from consciousness through having been forgotten or repressed, the contents of the collective unconscious have never been in consciousness, and therefore have never been individually acquired, but owe their existence exclusively to heredity. Whereas the personal unconscious consists for the most part of *complexes*, the content of the collective unconscious is made up essentially of *archetypes*."[3]

The realm of the unconscious is shown in Fig. 2 as the shaded portion occupying more than one half of the circle. If we think again of that vast expanse of land (Fig. 3), the tip of which is an island (consciousness and the ego) projecting above the water, the personal unconscious may be seen as a kind of "shadow land" stretching between consciousness and the unconscious that has not always been covered by the sea and can be reclaimed (e.g. repressed or forgotten experiences recalled and made conscious).

The personal unconscious belongs to the individual, whereas the collective unconscious belongs to the whole of humanity. It is inherited, inborn. We inherit it in a biological sense, through our brain structure, because the collective unconscious is "a universal and uniform substratum common to all humanity, because it is the historical background from which every mentality is evolved. . . . It is the soil formed by age-long deposits of mental processes in which the roots of the psyche are deeply imbedded . . . every experience passed through by man in his long ascent from lower forms of life has left its mark in the psyche; for even as physically the germ-cells pass unchanged from one generation to another, so traces of experience lived through ancestrally, and repeated millions of times, are imprinted in the structure of the brain, and, handed down through the centuries, reappear in dreams and in otherwise unaccountable reactions."[4]

The Sun, Moon and planets are associated with basic drives and archetypal patterns of behaviour, and each will have its characteristic functional connection with both the unconscious psyche and with consciousness. I can see no significant reason why the birthchart should be divided into the "unconscious half" (the first six houses below the horizon) and the "conscious half" (the last six houses above the horizon) as had been traditionally suggested. One might suggest that the five slowest-moving planets might symbolize unconscious activity rather than conscious activity, because due to the number of years each takes to transit a single sign of the zodiac their affects are most evidential (in terms of sign traits) as a background influence to a particular generation, to be interpreted collectively. This is true as far as effects on a given generation are concerned, but if we are to believe that each planet symbolizes particular archetypal processes which are contents of the collective unconscious, each planet will also symbolize the manifestations of these archetypes in terms of patterns of conscious mental behaviour.

The Archetypes

Archetypes manifest as patterns of emotional and mental behaviour in man. They are the dynamic contents and expressions of the collective unconscious, and as such they are common to all humanity. Jung has called them *primordial images*, which arise from the inherited foundations of the unconscious mind. "These archetypes, whose innermost nature is inaccessible to experience, represent the precipitate of psychic functioning of the whole ancestral line, i.e. the heaped-up, or pooled, experiences of organic existence in general, a million times repeated, and condensed into types. Hence, in these archetypes all experiences are represented which since primeval times have happened on this planet."[5]

Through our inheritance of the archetypal functions and contents of the collective unconscious we are inevitably linked to the very first life-striving of the primeval organism that has evolved into what we now call man or woman. We have inherited this built-up symbolic formula in a biological sense, through our brain structure, which has evolved out of the whole drama of human life experienced individually by our ancestors in an unbroken line from the beginnings of organic life itself.

Each dominant drive or desire in man has its archetypal compulsion and pattern of behaviour to direct him towards his goal. Man's reactions to danger, his experience of a "religious awakening", his need to gamble and speculate or to accumulate wealth and possessions—each is a product of an archetypal inheritance. "There are as many archetypes as there are typical situations in life. Endless repetition has engraved these experiences into our psychic constitution. . . . When a situation occurs which corresponds to a given archetype, that archetype becomes activated and a compulsiveness appears. . . ."[6]

Another way of understanding the archetypes is through their close similarity to what is probably far too loosely termed the *instincts* or *instinctive behaviour*. "Instincts are impersonal, universally distributed, hereditary factors of a dynamic or motivating character . . . the instincts are not vague and indefinite by nature, but are specifically formed motive forces which, long before there is any consciousness, and in spite of any degree of consciousness later on, pursue their inherent goals."[7] Jung has said that there is reason for supposing that the archetypes are the unconscious images of the instincts themselves. They are *patterns of instinctual behaviour*.

The Self

In Chapter 3 we will read how the Sun's symbol (☉) is the classic symbol for the unity and divinity of the self, and of the self as not only the centre but also the whole circumference which embraces both consciousness and unconscious. The self is the very centre of gravity of the individual. It is the archetypal process through which we seek self-realization. It is the focal point within us towards which all our highest and ultimate purposes seem to be striving. It is "a central point within the psyche, to which everything is related, by which everything is arranged, and which is itself a source of energy. The energy of the central point is manifested in the almost irresistible compulsion and urge to *become what one is*, just as every organism is driven to assume the form that is characteristic of its nature, no matter what the circumstances."[8]

Each planet must necessarily represent a psychic function that can be motivated by the purposeful activity of the self, and so be related to the self. Yet the concept of the self is most clearly symbolized by the Sun. Jupiter, Saturn, Neptune and Pluto can also be seen to represent vital archetypal processes for self-realization.

The Ego

The *ego* is that part of the conscious mind with which we normally identify ourselves. It is essentially the focal point of consciousness. It is aptly illustrated in Fig. 3 as an island jutting from the sea, depicting consciousness, self-consciousness, that has emerged from its origins in the unconscious which is that vast boundless area of land beneath the sea. Yet the ego itself is not exclusively conscious, but is a centre of reference, the core of a complex which projects more or less into consciousness but reaches also deep into the unconscious. As the most self-conscious part of the psyche we can see how the term *egocentric* applies to a person who is self-centred and concerned primarily with their own interests and being. The connection that most of the planets represent in terms of functional contribution to ego-development can be clearly seen.

The Persona

Originally, the *persona* was a mask worn by actors. Hence, the persona is a "complicated system of relations between the individual consciousness and society, fittingly enough a kind of mask, designed on the one hand to make a definite impression upon others, and, on the other, to conceal the true nature of the individual".[9] It is a compromise formation between the individual and society based on that which one appears to be—therefore being comprised of certain adopted attitudes expected of us by society, which simplify our contacts by also indicating what we may expect from other people. To quote Jung again, the persona is "the individual's system of adaptation to, or the manner he assumes in dealing with, the world. Every calling or profession, for example, has its own characteristic persona. . . . Only, the danger is that (people) become identical with their personas—the professor with his text-book, the tenor with his voice. . . . One could say, with a little exaggeration, that the persona is that which in reality one is not, but which oneself as well as others think one is."[10]

Each planet will contribute to the formation of the persona, in terms of the function the planet symbolizes in the psyche, though the Moon, Venus and Mars should indicate particularly evident features.

The Soul; Anima and Animus

The *soul*, in Jungian psychology and as it will be used in this book, refers to an inner personality, which is complementary to the outer personality or persona. Whereas the persona is an "outer attitude", a function mediating between the ego and the external world, the soul is an "inner attitude", a function mediating between the ego and the inner world of man. The male soul and the female soul are distinguished by the terms *anima* for a man and *animus* for a woman. Anima and animus are archetypes, and as such they are the foundation stones of the psychic structure, representing "*functions* which filter the contents of the collective unconscious through to the conscious mind".[11] They are one's inner attitude turned *towards* the unconscious, for the purpose of communicating the images of the unconscious to the conscious mind. "The animus and the anima should function as a bridge, or a door, leading to the images of the collective unconscious, as the persona should be a sort of bridge into the world."[12]

The anima is also the personification of the feminine nature, or latent feminine principal, of a man's unconscious; the animus is the masculine nature of a woman's unconscious. The anima has an erotic, emotional character, the animus a rationalizing one. "Every man carries within him the eternal image of woman, not the image of this or that particular

woman, but a definite feminine image. This image is fundamentally unconscious, an hereditary factor of primordial
origin engraved in the living organic system of the man, an
imprint or 'archetype' of all the ancestral experiences of the
female, a deposit, as it were, of all the impressions ever made
by woman."[13] And, like the anima, the animus in a woman
seems to be "derived from three roots: the collective image
of man which a woman inherits; her own experience of
masculinity coming through the contacts she makes with men
in her life; and the latent masculine principle in herself".[14]

Astrologically, the Moon, Mercury, Venus, Mars and
Uranus will tend to contribute (through the functions they
represent in the human psyche) significantly to the activities of
the anima and animus.

The Shadow

First and foremost the *shadow* represents the personal unconscious, that part of man containing complexes formed of
repressed desires and emotions. Jung has pointed out that
just as there can be no shadow without the Sun, so in the sense
of the personal unconscious there can be no shadow without
the light of consciousness. "The shadow is the inferior being in
ourselves, the one who wants to do all the things that we do
not allow ourselves to do, who is everything that we are not,
the Mr. Hyde to our Dr. Jekyll . . . the primitive, uncon-
trolled, and animal part of ourselves . . . all those uncivilized
desires and emotions that are incompatible with social standards and our ideal personality, all that we are ashamed of, all
that we do not want to know about ourselves."[15] But Jung
has indicated that although the shadow may appear to be
wholly a repressed and for the most part inferior and guilt-laden
personality, this is not entirely the case. The shadow "does
not consist only of morally reprehensible tendencies, but also
displays a number of good qualities, such as normal instincts,
appropriate reaction, realistic insights, creative impulses, etc."[16]

Obviously features of the shadow will not be easy to recognize in other people, or to admit in ourselves. Suspect behaviour
may be those occasions when we are "possessed" by an intense
emotion, overcome by a momentary uncontrollable rage, or

commit an offence against society for which we afterwards feel desperately ashamed. We may then find ourselves excusing our behaviour by saying, "I really don't know what came over me", or, "I was not myself". The field of investigation into the correlation of astrological factors with manifestations of shadow tendencies will hold many rewards for serious researchers. At present, the function related to Pluto appears theoretically to correlate with the natural process of shadow tendencies "coming to the surface", but other planets are likely to play significant roles according to the environmental circumstances which provoke or stimulate these otherwise hidden and repressed tendencies.

The Superior Function; Inferior Function

According to Jung there are four basic functions or forms of psychic activity present in every individual: thinking, feeling, sensation, and intuition. The functions of *thinking* and *feeling* are opposites, yet both are characterized as *rational* because they work with values: the thinking function judges and seeks an understanding of the world by means of thought and logical deductions, the feeling function is appreciation of values, a process that evaluates a given content on the basis of "like or dislike", "agreeable or disagreeable". The functions of *sensation* and *intuition* are also opposites, yet are characterized as *irrational* since they work with perceptions, without evaluation or interpretation: the sensation function perceives things as they are, what *is* in the present moment, whereas the intuition function perceives less through the conscious apparatus of the senses than through its capacity for an unconscious "inner perception" of the potentialities in things, and perceives the inner meaning of a thing or an occurrence.

Every individual adapts himself to reality most easily and most successfully by means of one of the four basic functions, called the *superior function*. Traits associated with this function will predominate and will determine the individual's *type*. By the law of opposites, as an inherent principle of human nature, the opposite function to the superior function will be the *inferior function*. This function is believed to lie wholly in the unconscious and to be entirely beyond the disposal of the will.

It belongs to the things that happen to one completely independent of one's conscious intention. "It breaks in upon you autonomously from the unconscious whenever it pleases. Being intermingled with the unconscious wholly without differentiation, it has an infantile, primitive, instinctive, archaic character. Therefore we are so often surprised by actions of a moody, savage, passionate kind proceeding from persons to whose nature as we know it they seem completely foreign."[17]

Astrologically, the superior function should be determined by strongly emphasized factors in the birth-chart, possibly by the sign the Sun or the Ascendant are placed in. An important line of research needs to be undertaken to find whether the theoretically strongest factor/factors in a given birth-chart do always predictably correlate with the most dominant and expected traits. These factors would be likely to indicate the type of superior function, and lead to an understanding of the subject's inferior function.

NOTES

1. *Psychological Types*, by Carl Jung, p. 588 (Routledge & Kegan Paul, Ltd.).
2. *The Psychology of Jung*, by Jolan Jacobi, p. 9 (Routledge & Kegan Paul, Ltd.).
3. *The Archetypes and the Collective Unconscious*, by Carl Jung, p. 42 (Routledge & Kegan Paul, Ltd.).
4. *ABC of Jung's Psychology*, by Joan Corrie, p. 15 (Kegan Paul, Trench, Trubner & Co. Ltd.).
5. *Psychological Types*, by Carl Jung, p. 507 (Routledge & Kegan Paul, Ltd.).
6. *The Archetypes and the Collective Unconscious*, by Carl Jung, p. 48 (Routledge & Kegan Paul, Ltd.).
7. *Ibid.*, p. 43.
8. *Ibid.*, p. 337.
9. *Two Essays on Analytical Psychology*, by Carl Jung, p. 192 (Routledge & Kegan Paul, Ltd.).
10. *The Archetypes and the Collective Unconscious*, p. 122 (Routledge & Kegan Paul, Ltd.).
11. *Aion*, by Carl Jung, p. 20 (Routledge & Kegan Paul, Ltd.).
12. "Unpublished Seminar Notes by Carl Jung", *Visions*, I, p. 116.
13. *The Development of Personality*, by Carl Jung, p. 198 (Routledge & Kegan Paul, Ltd.).
14. *An Introduction to Jung's Psychology*, by Frieda Fordham, p. 55 (Pelican Books).
15. *Ibid.*, pp. 49–50.
16. *Aion*, by Carl Jung, p. 266 (Routledge & Kegan Paul, Ltd.).
17. *The Psychology of Jung*, by Jolan Jacobi, p. 16 (Routledge & Kegan Paul, Ltd.).

11   *Food for Thought*

A great deal of extremely interesting research has been reported on in recent years to indicate that not only the Sun and the Moon but the planets also have significant effects on terrestrial life—including humans. To quote even fairly briefly from all the reports that I have copies of would probably fill the equivalent of several more chapters. Therefore I will quote just a few, and include some interesting comments made by qualified persons. These are taken at random from my files and are not given in any particular order. Interested readers should make their own collection of reports from scientific sources, where these concern physiological clocks, and the affects of the Moon or the planets on any form of organic life or weather phenomena, and the correlation of sunspots with life on our planet.

The late John J. O'Neill, Science Editor of the *New York Herald-Tribune*, in a letter dated 8 July 1951, stated: "The hypothesis of the astrologers that forces are transmitted without attenuation with increasing distance, and do not vary with respect to the difference in masses of the sun, moon, and planets on which they originate, was totally inconsistent with the old style Newtonian mechanics; but today is in complete accord with the much more recent Einstein photo-electric theory, which demonstrates that the effect of a photon does not diminish with distance, and which has been universally adopted by scientists to supplant the Newtonian mechanics in that field.

"The hypothesis of the astrologers that different effects will be produced by different configurations of the heavenly bodies, is entirely consistent with the modern developments in the field of chemistry, in which the properties of substances are stated in terms of architectural configurations of the atoms within the molecules, and with the theories of the atomic physicists that the properties of the atoms are associated with the orbital architecture of the electrons."

"The human living on the planet Earth is governed more by the motion of celestial bodies than scientists think. . . . Intermediate between the two extremes of heavy, slow celestial bodies governed by gravitational forces, and electrons in atoms, humans are both made of, and have to live in, electromagnetic forces, fields, and waves." (From *ISA Transactions*, Vol. 8, No. 4, 1969, published by the Instrument Society of America, Pittsburgh, Pa.)

The following correlations with the Moon's phases are reported in *Cycles in Your Life*, by Darrell Huff (Victor Gollancz Ltd., London, 1965). "It has been noted, in parts of South America and on South Sea islands, that timber felled at the time of the waxing moon is abnormally full of sap" (*page 38*). "An electrical potential in maple trees, of varying direction and voltage, has been found to follow regular cycles which seem to correlate with the Moon's phases" (*page 39*). "Dr. Frank A. Brown, Jr., a North-western University biologist, experimented with a piece of potato, sealing it in a chamber where it was kept under constant pressure, temperature, light, and humidity. Yet living under such baffling conditions the bit of potato was able to predict what the atmospheric pressure outside its sealed chamber would be two days later—its metabolic rate or consumption of oxygen correlated inversely with the barometer reading two days afterwards. The metabolic rate of the piece of potato was lowest at the time of the New Moon and highest during the third quarter" (*page 39*). "At Northwestern University, Professor Frank A. Brown found that how a worm turns, whether to the left or to the right, corresponds to which phase the moon is in" (*page 112*). "Dr. Leonard J. Ravitz has measured differences in electrical voltage between human heads and chests. The differences change from day to day in cycles that correspond to Moon phases" (*page 112*). "The Philadelphia Police Department made a report in 1961 to the American Institute of Medical Climatology on the 'Effect of Full Moon on Human Behaviour'. Their conclusion: 'People whose antisocial behaviour had psychotic roots—such as firebugs,

kleptomaniacs, destructive drivers, and homicidal alcoholics—
seemed to go on a rampage as the moon rounded, calming
down as the moon waned'" (*page 113*). "A Florida surgeon,
an ear-nose-throat man, has found remarkably clear evidence
of a moon cycle in bleeding. Reporting in the *Journal* of the
Florida Medical Association, Dr. Edson J. Andrews, of Talla-
hassee, tells what he found when he plotted cases of excessive
post-operative bleeding against the cycles of the moon.
Working with more than a thousand cases, and defining
'bleeders' as patients requiring unusual means of hemostasis
on the operating table or requiring return to the operating
room because of hemorrhaging, he found . . . a great pre-
ponderance of bleeders near the time of the full moon and
only an insignificant number at the new moon. In the interval
between the first quarter and one day before the third quarter,
82 per cent of all the cases occurred. 'What makes this observation even more astounding,' says Dr. Andrews, 'is the fact that
there were fewer admissions during the time of the full moon....
These data have been so conclusive and convincing to me, I
threaten to become a witch doctor and operate on dark nights
only, saving the moonlit nights for romance'" (*page 114*).
"Controller Curtis Jackson, at the Methodist Hospital of
Southern California in Los Angeles, studied 11,007 birth
records covering a six-year period. He found a 29·5-day cycle
in births, and the evidence pointed to more babies being born
at the time of the Full Moon than at New Moon. Some years
earlier, Dr. W. Buehler in Freiburg, Bavaria, made a similar
study of 33,000 births. He found the same 29·5-day wave
paralleling the Moon's phases" (*page 115*). "A Chicago
physician, Dr. W. F. Petersen, found that deaths in Chicago
from tuberculosis occurred most frequently seven days after
Full Moon and reached a low eleven days before Full Moon.
There is, he says, a lunar cycle in terrestrial magnetism, terrestrial temperature, and variation of blood pH (degree of
acidity or alkalinity)" (*page 116*).

From numerous sources one can read of correlations being
found or suspected between sunspot numbers and terrestrial
affairs and cycles of activity in organic life. A very good source
is *Sunspots and Their Effects*, by H. T. Stetson (The Scientific

Book Club). The following is a list from various authoritative sources of correlations with sunspot numbers of considerable significance. To detail these would take up far too much space: tree rings, wine harvests, migration of birds, booms and depressions in business, levels of the River Nile and the Great Lakes, rainfall, abundance of cod and mackerel, mass human reactions to leaders and mass human movements in history, human disease and suicide, animal populations, abundance of pelts of the fox and the lynx and the rabbit, biennial atmospheric oscillation, monsoon storms, barometric pressure, sunshine, terrestrial temperature, climatic fluctuation, hailstorms, formation of bloodclots in individuals so disposed, pulmonary disease, tuberculosis deaths, epidemics of diphtheria, cholera, typhus and smallpox, chemical reactions, migration pattern of locust, radio reception.

With solar radiations undoubtedly influencing terrestrial life, the question has arisen as to whether the positions of the planets act as a "trigger" to the main cause for the eruptions (spots) on the Sun's surface. Evidence is mounting that this is so. With the planets contributing to the formation of sunspots and fluctuations in solar radiation, they would also be contributing to the Sun's effects on terrestrial life, and as was said in the *New Scientist* of 21 October 1965, "if this picture of events is established it could, of course, lead to accurate predictions of solar activity". And the prediction of the various solar affects upon life on Earth.

Three New York scientists, Howard Friedman, Charles H. Bachman, and Robert O. Becker, recorded the number of daily admissions in eight large New York psychiatric hospitals and compared these with the hour by hour magnetic activity of the Sun. During the period under study, from 1 July 1957 to 30 October 1961, there were 28,642 admissions. The statistical analysis clearly shows that admissions increase on days of strongest magnetic disturbance. The authors' conclusions were: "The results are in keeping with the conception of the behaviour of an organism being significantly influenced through the direct current control system, by external force fields. Attention is thus invited to a hitherto neglected dimension in the complexity of psychopathology specifically, and perhaps generally in all human behavior."

"Water is not only the liquid of our earth, it is also the liquid of our lives. Living organisms are exposed to the cosmos as the colloids in their laboratory beakers are. Cosmic forces act upon them through the mediation of the water contained in their bodies. The human body, for instance, is 65 per cent water. Water is found in blood, in the lymph, in every organ of our body. Several chemists, Magat in particular, have shown that the structure of water is especially precarious at the normal temperature of the human body. It is in fact between 35 to 40 degrees Centigrade that water definitely loses its structure to become a perfect liquid" (Michel Gauquelin: *The Cosmic Clocks*, p. 220). "Perhaps it is even by means of water and the aqueous system that the external forces are able to react on living organisms" (G. Piccardi: *The Chemical Basis of Medical Climatology*, Springfield, Ill.: Charles Thomas, 1962). And Michel Gauquelin (of the Psychophysiological Laboratory at Strasbourg University) in *Astrology and Science* (Peter Davies, London, 1970), comments on the Piccardi experiments with water: "So space and cosmic forces can affect us through the intermediary of water. That is a conclusion of formidable importance. In fact, water is all over the earth, it is the planet's major liquid. The whole of physics and the whole of chemistry must take into account the variations which the structure of water undergoes, as do the pyramids of molecules submitted to continuous alteration, distortion and pressures, according to the earth's trajectory and the cosmic forces which reverberate against it."

"Gravitation enters everywhere; there is nothing on earth that can escape its effects. . . . All living things, no matter how small, react in each of their cells to the gravitational pull that follows from the movements of the sun and of the moon" (Michel Gauquelin: *The Cosmic Clocks*, p. 143, Henry Regnery Co., Chicago, 1967).

In 1962 three American research workers, Donald A. Bradley and M. A. Woodbury of New York University, and G. W. Brier of Massachusetts Institute of Technology, disclosed their study of the relationship between the Moon's phases and rainfall, based on a statistical analysis of rainfall records from 1,544 weather stations during the fifty years from 1900 to 1949. They reported: "It can be stated that, when dates of excessive precipitation are plotted in terms of the angular difference between the moon and sun, a pronounced departure from normal expectancy becomes conspicuous. There is a marked tendency for extreme precipitation in North America to be recorded near the middle of the first and third weeks of the synodical month, especially on the third to fifth days after the configurations of both new and full moon. The second and fourth quarters of the lunation cycle are correspondingly deficient in heavy precipitation, the low point falling about 3 days previous to the date of the alignment of the earth-moon-sun system" ("Lunar Synodical Period and Widespread Precipitation", in *Science*, CXXXVII, 1962, p. 748). Unknown to the Americans, two Australian researchers, E. E. Adderley and E. G. Bowen of the Radiophysics Division of the Commonwealth Scientific and Industrial Research Organization in Sydney, had arrived independently at similar results based on rainfall observations from fifty weather stations in New Zealand from 1901–25. Two years later, in 1964, Donald A. Bradley took the records of 269 Atlantic hurricanes between 1899 and 1958, and noted the positions of the Moon when they "matured", that is, when they first developed winds of force 12 on the meteorologist's Beaufort scale. He found that 90 of the hurricanes matured within 46 hours of either New Moon or Full Moon. As that is 20 or more than the expectancy if there was no connection between hurricanes and the lunar cycle the result is, in statistician's terms, highly significant.

A German geophysicist, Rudolph Tomaschek, Professor of Theoretical Physics at the University of Munich, examined 134 severe earthquakes (above an index of 7·75) occurring between 1904–52. He found that during each of these earthquakes the planet Uranus (which astrologers associate with seismological activity) was within plus or minus 15° of the upper or lower meridian.

"Dr. Harold Burr, emeritus professor of anatomy at Yale University School of Medicine, states that what establishes the pattern of a particular human brain, and 'regulates and controls' it, is actually a complex magnetic field. The human central nervous system, he says, is a superb receptor of electromagnetic energies, the finest in all nature—with 10,000 million brain cells, it has a myriad of possible circuits through which electricity can channel. It is quite possible, therefore, that in a manner not yet discovered, earthly magnetic fields may influence human behaviour, their rhythmic ebb and flow producing within our brains cyclical changes in feeling, alertness and sensibility, perhaps even stirring the memory or inciting ideas" (Rutherford Platt: "Outer Space and the Tides of Life", in *The Reader's Digest*, May 1963).

Dr. Bolton, head of the Psychiatric Department at Temple University: "It has long been accepted by psychiatrists that the moon is known to have a serious effect on the minds of persons afflicted with nervous disorders."

Is it not astonishing that each man and woman does not instinctively accept that this great fiery source of all energy and light, the Sun, let alone the Moon and the planets, must affect human behaviour? "Life, wherever it exists, is a product of starlight. All life on earth feeds on radiation coming from a yellow and middle-aged star which we call the sun. The energy of sunlight becomes life through the mediation of plant and animal cells. The essential operation involved consists of changing energy from one form to another—specifically, transforming radiant energy from the sun into the chemical energy which enables the single cell to thrive and multiply, the tree to flourish, the tiger to stalk its prey and man to write his history in the stars" (*The Cell*, by John Pfeiffer, p. 30, Time-Life Books, 1969).

Finally, to return again to the late John J. O'Neill, whom we quoted at the beginning of this chapter. He was the only science writer ever to win a Pulitzer Prize for his work. He was Science Editor for the *New York Herald-Tribune*, and at one time condemned astrology as utterly unscientific and irrational. Apparently in making a study of astrology for the purpose of proving how absurd the subject was, he came to believe in it. The American magazine, *Analog Science Fact*, quoted portions of a letter written by O'Neill in support of an astrologer: "I speak as a scientist who does not deviate to the slightest degree from the most rigorous adherence to the highest standards of demonstrated evidence in support of truth. I do deviate from the average attitude of scientists in that I place far more reliance on direct observation of nature than I place on textbooks and human authorities. . . . Astrology is one of the most important fields for scientific research today, and one of the most neglected. Astrology, properly defined, is the science of the relationship of man and his celestial environment; it is the accumulated and organized knowledge of the effect on man of the forces reaching the earth from surrounding space. . . . There is absolutely nothing unscientific about engaging in research in this field, and no stigma of any kind should be associated with it in the mind of any scientist or layman. . . . Scientists today cannot look down on astrology; instead, they must raise their eyes to take in the higher horizons that astrologers have preserved for them. . . . Attacks on astrology, without previous extensive investigations by competent individuals must, from now on, be regarded as a very antiquated, unscientific practice closely related to witch hunting, and must be correctly diagnosed as a symptom of professional paranoia on the part of the individual doing the attacking."

APPENDIX I

The Planets and Vegetation

Traditionally, the Sun, the Moon and each planet is said to have a significant association with particular plants, shrubs and trees. There seems little doubt that for centuries those plants and trees, but particularly herbs, known to possess medicinal properties to combat human sickness and disease have been considered of prime importance by astrologers interested in this field of study.

The connection between a particular plant and a particular planet seems in most cases to be decided by the nature of the remedy provided by the plant, the types of human ailments it is said to provide relief or a cure for, and the planet that is associated with these types of ailment. Herbs are used as remedies on the principles of *sympathy* or *antipathy*. For instance, Mars by nature is inflammatory, eruptive, and fever-promoting; Saturn by nature is cooling, binding, and fever-reducing. Thus disorders and diseases connected with (traditionally it would be said "caused by") Mars may be combated by the herbs and remedies of Saturn *by antipathy*. Or, if the herbs and remedies of Mars are used, *by sympathy*.

One cannot help feeling, however, that in a number of cases a plant has been placed "under the rulership" of a particular planet simply because its name or a certain feature of its growth seems most aptly connected with that planet, and without any justifiable evidence to support this theory. For instance, "all sweet-smelling spices and perfumes" are said to be connected with Venus, whilst "thorny and prickly trees" are said to be associated with Mars. The study of the relationship between the planets and vegetation is still in its infancy: what a vast subject for keen young researchers to specialize in.

In the following lists there are a few occasions where the

same plant is stated to be connected with more than one planet. My own reasoning would say that *each* plant or tree has a connection more or less with the Sun, Moon and *every* planet, though probably there would be found to be a specially significant association with just one of these bodies.

The Sun (☉)

Almond, Anagallis Arvensis, Angelica Sylvestris, Anise, Anthemis Nobillis, Ash tree, Bay tree, Calendula Officinalis, Cedar tree, Celandine, Centaurea Nigra, Chamomile, Chelidonium Majus, Cinnamon, Citrus Aurantium Colchicum Autumnale, Corn Hornwort, Daffodil, Drosera Rotundifolia, Echium Vulgare, Euphrasia Chamomilla, Eyebright, Fernel, Frankincense, Fraxinus Excelsior, Grape (Vitis Vinifera), Heart Trefoil, Helianthus, Hypericum Androsaemium, Juniperus Communis, Laurel, Lavender, Lemon, Ligusticum Scoticum, Maize, Male Peony, Marigold, Meadow Rue, Mistletoe, Musk, Mustard, Olive, Orange, Palm tree, Passion Flower, Pennyroyal, Peony, Peppermint, Petasites Vulgaris, Pimpernel, Poppy (Yellow), Potentilla Tormentilla, Rice, Rosmarinus Officinalis, Rue, Saffron, Sage, Sanguisorba Officinalis, Sinapis Nigra and Alba, St. John's Wort, St. Peter's Wort, Sundew, Sun-flower, Tormentil, Turnsole, Vervain, Vine (Vitis Vinifera), Viper's Bugloss, Walnut tree. All aromatic herbs.

The Moon (☽)

Acunthus Mollis, Adder's Tongue, Agaricus, Anthemis Pyrethrum, Betony Stone-crop, Brassicae, Buck's Meat, Cabbage, Caltrops, Cardamine Pratensis, Cauliflower, Cherianthus Cheiri, Chickweed, Clary, Cleavers Coralwort, Colewort, Colocynth, Convolvulus Coeruleus, Cress, Cuckoo Flowers, Cucumbers, Cucumis Sativis, Cucurbito Pepo, Common Daisy, Daisy Dogtooth, Duck's Meat, Duckweed, Endive, Geranium Triste, Gourd, Honeysuckle, Hyssop, Iris, Kale, Lactucas, Ladysmock, Lemnae, Lettuces, Livelong, Loosestrife, Meadow Lily, Melon, Mercurialis Annua, Mercury, Moonwort, Mouse-ear, Mushrooms, Ophioglossum Vulgatum, Orpine, Palm tree, Pearlwort, Pellitory, Peplis Portula, Poppy,

Portulaca Oleraceae, Potato, Privet, Pumpkin, Purslane, Pyrethrum, Rattle Grass, Rosemary, Salices, Salvia Verbenaca, Saxifrage (Winter), Seaweeds, Spunk, Stellaria Media, Stonecrop, Trefoil, Turnip, Utricularia Vulgaris, Wallflowers, Water Arrowhead, Watercress, Waterflag, Water Lily (yellow), Water Violet, White Lily, White Poppy, White Rose, White Saxifrage, Whitlow Grass, Wild Wallflower, Willow trees, Wintergreen, Woodbine. Trees which are mostly rich in sap, and night-growing plants.

Mercury (☿)

Amara-Dulcis, Anethum Graveolens, Anise, Aniseed, Apium Gravolens, Artemisia Abrotantum, Avena, Azaleas, Balm (or Melissa), Barberry, Bitter Sweet, Bryonia Alba, Calamintha Officinalis, Caraway, Carrots, Carum Carui, Celery, Convallaria Majalis, Coraline, Corylus Avellana, Cow Parsnip, Cynoglossum Officinale, Daffodils, Daucus Carota, Dill, Elder tree, Elecampane, Elfwort, Endive, Fennel, Fern, Flax, Foeniculum Vulgare, Germander, Glycerrhiza Glabra and Enchinata, Hare's Foot, Hazelnut tree, Horehound (White), Hound's Tongue, Inula Helenium, Lavandula Vera, Lilac tree, Lily of the Valley, Liquorice, May Apple, Maidenhair (White and Golden), Male Fern, Mandrake, Marjoram (Common, Wild, and Sweet), Medlar, Myrtle, Nailwort, Nephrodium Felix Mas, Nux Vomica, Oats, Olive Spurge, Organum Vulgare, Parietaria Officinalis, Parsley (Wild), Pastinaca Sativa, Pellitory of the Wall, Petroselinum Sativum, Podophyllin, Pomegranates, Quince, Satureia Hortensis, Savory, Savoy, Scabiosa Succisa, Smallage, Southern Wood, Starwort, Succory, Tansy, Teucrium Scorodonia, Trefoil, Valerian, Walnut tree, Wild Carrots, Winter Savory. All plants whose medicines remove obstructions.

Venus (♀)

Acillea Ptarmica, Ajuga Reptans, Alder tree (Black and Common), Alehoof, Alkanet, Almond tree, Alnus Glutinosa, Althaea Officinalis, Apple trees, Apricot tree, Archangel (Wild and Stinking), Arctium Lappa, Arrack, Artichoke, Ash tree, Asparagus, Beans, Bear Berry, Bellis Perennis, Birch tree, Bishop's Weed, Blites, Brambles, Bugle Holly, Bunium

Flexuosum, Burdock, Cherry trees, Chestnut trees, Chickpease, Cloves, Cock's-Head, Coltsfoot, Columbines, Couchgrass, Cowslip, Crabsclaw, Cranesbill, Crosswort, Cudweed, Cypress tree, Daffodils, Daisy, Dandelion, Devil's-Bit, Dipsacus Sylvestris, Dropwort, Elder tree, Eryngium Maritimum, Featherfew, Ferns, Fig tree, Figwort, Forget-Me-Not, Foxglove, Fumitory, Galium Cruciatum, Golden Rod, Gooseberry, Grapes and other Vines, Gromel, Groundsel, Hawthorn tree. Herb Robert, Holly (Sea), Ivy (Ground), Indigo Plant, Kidney Bean, Kidney Wort, Ladies' Bedstraw, Ladies' Mantle, Leonurus Cardiaca, Ligustrum Vulgare, Lilies, Lithospermum Arvense, Little Daisy, Mallow (Common), Marshmallow, Matricaria Parthenium, Mentha Pulegium, Mercury (Dog and French), Meum Athamanticum, Mint-Money-Wort, Mints, Motherwort, Mugwort, Myrtle, Nepeta Cataria, Nepeta Glechoma, Obione Portulacoides, Okro Gombo Pods, Orchis, Oxalis Acetosella, Pansies, Parsley, Peach tree, Pear tree, Penny Royal, Pennywort, Peppermint, Plantago Major, Plantain (Greater), Plum trees, Pomegranate tree, Poppy (White), Primula Veris, Prunella Vulgaris, Pulsatilla, Queen of the Meadows, Ragwort, Red Cherries, Roses (especially Damask), Rubus Fruticosis, Rye, Sanicle, Sanicula Europaea, Saponaria Officinalis, Scrophularia Nodosa and Aquatica, Secale Cereale, Selfheal, Senecio Jacobaea, Sibthorpia Europaea, Silverweed, Snowdrop, Soapwort, Sinchus Arvensis, Sorrel, Sowthistle, Spearmint, Spignel, Strawberry, Tansy, Teasel, Throatwort, Thyme, Tussilago Farfara, Verbena Officinalis, Vervain, Violets, Wheat, Yarrow. All sweet-smelling spices and perfumes.

Mars (♂)

Ajuva Chamaepitys, All-heal, Allium Sativum, Aloes, Anenome, Arnica, Arsmart, Artemisia Absinthium, Arum Maculatum, Barberry, Basil, Bayberry, Berberis Vulgaris, Box tree, Briars, Briony, Brooklime, Broom, Broomrape, Bryonia Dioica, Buckthorn, Butcher's Broom, Cacti, Capsicum, Capers, Carduus Benedictus, Cassia Obovata, Catmint, Cayenne Pepper, Centaurea Calcipitra, Centaury (American), Cinchona, Civet, Cochlearia Armoracia, Coffee, Corlander,

Cotton Thistle, Cranesbill (Wild), Crataegus Oxyacantha, Cresses, Crowfoot (Marsh), Daisy (English), Dock, Dove's-foot, Dragon's Flaxweed, Dyer's-weed, Furze Bush, Garden Cress, Garlic, Gentian (Yellow), Geranium Robertianum and Columbinum, Ginger, Gratriola Officinalis, Hawthorn, Hemlock, Hemp, Holly tree, Honeysuckle, Hope, Hops, Horehound, Horse-radish, Horse-tongue, Humulus Lupus, Hyssop (Hedge), Juniperus Sabina, Lead Wort, Leeks, Linum (various species of), Madder, Masterwort, Mousetail, Mustard, Myrtle (Wax), Nettles (small stinging), Ocymum Basilicum, Onions, Oregon Grappe, Peppers, Peppermint, Peruvian Bark, Peucedanum Ostruthium, Pine trees, Pineapple, Plantain, Poison Nut, Quaker Button, Radish, Ranunculus Aquatilis, Rheum Rhaponticum and Undulatum, Rhubarb, Rocket, Rubia Tinctorum, Sarsaparilla, Savin, Senna (Alexandrian), Sisymbrium Sophia, Smilax, Snake Root (White), Star Thistle, Strychnos Nux Vomica, Tea, Thistle (Lady's), Tobacco, Ulex Europaeus, Urtica (Urens, Dioica, and Pilulifera), Valeriana Officinalis, Vermouth, Wakerobin, Witch-hazel, Wormwood (Common). All thorny and prickly trees and shrubs.

Jupiter (♃)

Acer Campestre, Agrimonia Eupatoria, Alexander, Aloe (American), Almond tree, Aniseed, Apricots, Asclepias Vincetoxicum, Ash tree, Asparagus Officinalis, Avens, Balm, Balsam, Beet (White), Beta Vulgaris, Betonica Officinalis, Betony, Bilberry, Birch tree, Bloodwort, Borago Officinalis (Borage), Carnations, Castanea Vesca, Chaerophyllum Sativum, Chervil, Chestnut trees, Cichorium Endivia, Cinnamon, Cinquefoil, Cloves, Cochlearia Officinalis, Columbine, Costmary, Crithmum Maritumum, Currants, Daisies, Dandelion, Dianthus Caryophyllus, Dock, Dog Grass, Elm tree, Endive, Eupatorium, Ficus Carica, Fig Tree, Flag (Blue), Foxglove, Fumitoria Officinalis, Geum Urbanum, Gilliflowers, Ginseng, Hart's Tongue, Hissopus Officinalis (Hyssop), Houseleek, Iris, Jasmine, Jessamine, Lapsana Communis, Larkspur, Leek, Lichen Caninus and Islandicus, Lime tree, Linden tree, Liverwort, Lungwort, Mallow, Maple tree, Marchantia Polymorpha, Melilotus Officinalis, Melissa Officinalis, Melitot, Mints, Moss

(Iceland), Mulberry tree, Myrrh, Nailwort, Nutmegs, Oak tree, Olive tree, Parsnip, Peppermint, Periwinkle, Pinks (Wild), Polybody, Potentilla Reptans, Pulmonaria Officinalis, Rhubarb, Roses (Red), Saccharum Officinalis, Sage, Salvia Officinalis, Scurvy Grass, Sempervivium Tectorum, Small Samphire, Smyrnium Olusatrum, Strawberries, Succory (Wild), Sugar Cane, Swallow-wort, Tanacetum Vulgare, Taraxacum Densleonus (Dandelion), Thistle, Thorn Apple, Thyme, Tomato, Tormentil, Triticum Repens, Turnips, Vaccinium Myrtillus.

Saturn ($\hbar$)

Aconite, Aegopodium, Amaranthus Blitum, Aspen tree, Asplenium Ceterach, Atropa Belladonna, Barley, Barrenwort, Beech tree, Beet, Belladonna, Birdsfoot, Bistort, Black Alder tree, Black Hellebore, Blackthorn, Blue Bottle, Boneset, Buckthorn, Cannabis Sativa, Capsella Bursa-pastoris, Carduus Heterophyllus, Centaurea Nigra, Clown's Woundwort, Comfrey, Conium Maculatum, Crosswort, Cydonia Vulgaris, Cypress tree, Deadly Nightshade, Digitalis, Elm tree, Equisetum Vulgaris, Fagus Sylvatica, Flaxweed, Fleawort, Fumitory, Gladwin, Goutwort, Ground Moss, Hawkweed, Heartsease, Hedera Helix, Helleborus Niger, Hemlock, Hemp (Indian), Henbane, Holly tree, Hordeum Species, Horsetail, Hyoscyamus Niger, Ilex Aquifolium, Illecebrum Verticillatum, Isatis Tinctoria, Ivy (Common), Jew's Ear, Knapweed, Knotgrass, Lolium Parenne, Mandrake, Mangel, Medlar, Mespilus Germanica, Mosses, Mullein (Great), Navelwort, New Jersey Tea, Oak tree, Onions, Ornithopus Perpusillus, Pansies, Parsnip, Persicaria Urens, Pine trees, Plantago Psyllium, Plantain (Plantago), Polygonatum Multiflorum, Polypod (Rock), Polypodium Dryopteris, Poplar (Aspen) tree, Poppy, Populus Nigra, Potato, Prunus Spinosa, Purus Torminalis, Quince, Rhus Toxicodendron, Rue, Rupture Wort, Rushes, Rye, Sciatica Wort, Senna, Service tree, Shepherd's Purse, Sloes, Solomon's Seal, Spinach, Spleenwort, Symphytum Officianlis, Tamarix Anglica, Taxus Baccata, Thistles, Tulsan, Ulmus Campestris, Verbascum Thapsus, Vervain, Willow tree, Wintergreen, Wolfsbane, Yew tree.

Uranus (♅)

Uncertain, though of the herbs, Croton Oil, the oil from the seed of the Croton Tiglium tree, is said to be probably typical. Manly Palmer Hall suggests that the plants may be of the nature of those associated with the Moon and Venus.

Neptune (♆)

Is said to have a connection with herbs which are of a narcotic, soporific and sleep-producing, anaesthetic nature, such as Opiates, Tobacco, Cocaine, Heroin, Morphine. The Poppy from which opium is made. Cocaine is the alkaloid taken from the Coca plant (Cuca), or Erythroxylon Coca. Coffee possibly. Mushrooms and Fungoids would seem to be definitely associated with Neptune, also Mosses have been suggested. Manly Palmer Hall suggests that the plants may be similar to those connected with the Sun and Mercury.

Pluto (♇)

No known connections.

APPENDIX II

Vocation

The following are the traditional designations of vocations said to be associated with the Sun, Moon or planets respectively. The theory is that a planet strongly placed in a chart does not mean that the subject *should* or *will* take up one of the careers or types of work listed under that planet, but that the traits associated with that planet would be apt or beneficial should any of these employments be followed. Many of the occupations listed will no doubt cause the reader to be amused. However, I have not attempted to include selections from the multiple vocations one can choose from today, but faithfully record those of, shall we say, historical interest.

Sun: jeweller, goldsmith, banker, courtier, gilder, Government and Civil Service employees, managerial or executive, foreman, Stock Exchange, a leader or one having considerable authority.

Moon: hospital staff and Health Department workers, obstetrician, gynaecologist, the Navy, fishing industry, to do with liquids, bath-house proprietor, boat builders and designers, laundry work, traveller, salesman, advertising, estate agent, building trade, catering and hotel industry, plastics, public transport, baker, dairy farming, milkman, mushroom grower, gardener or horticulturalist, cheese manufacturing, chicken farmer or distributor, chinaware and glassware industry.

Mercury: writer, publishing, advertising, bookseller, journalist, general clerical work, secretary, printer, stationer, paper manufacturer, accountant, educational field (especially teaching), interpreter, linguist, orator, interviewer, radio or television announcer or commentator, compére, disc jockey, solicitor, lawyer, Post Office employees, road and rail transport, salesman and representative, middle-man, distributor of goods, agent, merchant, ambassador, sculptor, mathematician, architect, draughtsman, juggler, magician, retail grocery, buyer, neurologist.

Venus: all artistic work—music, painting, acting, ballet, entertainer; florist, landscape gardener, art museum curator, photography, confectionery, catering, wine trade, interior decorator, cashier, furniture manufacturer or dealer, upholsterer, tailoring, the "rag trade", perfumer, cosmetics, jeweller, hairdresser or stylist, beauty parlour, draughtsman, engraver, illustrator, fashion designer.

Mars: the Army, Police Force, surgeon or physician, dentist, cutler, butcher, tanner, carpenter, blacksmith, ironmonger, iron and steel industry, armament manufacturer, gunsmith, mechanic, technician, machinist, fireman, hardware trade, lumberjack, athletics, boxer, wrestler.

Jupiter: Legal profession, physician, chiropodist, banker, financier, insurance, Stock Exchange, clergy, theologian, philosopher, linguist, academics, Civil Service, Government, local government, philanthropist, charity work, scientist generally, diplomatic service, commerce, woollen merchant and provision dealers generally, publishing, courier, shoe trade, referee, sports goods industry, golfer, archer, horse racing—jockey, trainer, owner, turf commission agent or employee.

Saturn: coal-mining industry, coal merchant, excavator, plumber, labourer, potter, estate agent, agriculture and horticulture, building industry, cement industry, junk dealer, leather-goods industry, chimney sweep, architect, dealer in lead, antiquarian, prison employee, ice-cream industry, monk, nun, grave-digger, undertaker, horologist, historian.

Uranus: Air Force, aeronautics, astrologer, scientific field, research worker, historian, antiquarian, electronics industry, physics, computers, telegraphy, radio and television industry, electrical industry, photographic industry, cinema employee, inventor, engineering, social service and welfare, radiology, Civil Service.

Neptune: chemical industry, hospital staff (especially

anaesthetist), social welfare, animal welfare, the liquor trade, oil industry, the Arts, tobacco industry, diver, distiller, artiste, spiritual medium or healer, magician, occultist.

Pluto: undertaker, embalmer, grave-digger, all types of mining, oil industry, underground pipe manufacturer, detective or private investigator, psychiatrist, psychologist.

APPENDIX III

Colours

The following list of colours associated with the Sun, Moon and planets have not been compiled for the purpose of satisfying the curiosity of any reader whose interest in astrology is still on the fortune-telling level, but as a straightforward presentation of evidence as to how confused and nonsensical many astrologers past and present can be in their applications of astrology. My sources of reference have been the textbooks or writings of a very large number of mostly well-known astrologers. The generally accepted colours associated with a planet are given first, followed by other colours and shades attributed to the same planet. It may well be true, and ultimately proven by qualified scientific investigators, that certain colours do have a subtle connection with the cosmic bodies, but one wonders how much listed below is wild speculation! Shades of blue, for instance, are attributed to the Sun, Moon, Mercury, Venus, Jupiter, Saturn, Uranus and Neptune!

Sun: orange, gold, yellow-brown; also, all shades of brown, blue, yellow-purple, deep hues of yellow, amber, ermine, saffron.

Moon: green, silver, white, silver-grey; also, iridescent silvery hues, straw-yellow, pale yellowish-white, white spotted, delicate pastel shades just off white, lemon, cream, buff, fawn, grey, pearl, pale blue, purple, violet, opal, spotted and mixed colours.

Mercury: violet, slate, azure-blue, pink; also, dove-grey, blue-grey, pale-grey, spotted mixtures, plaids, checks, cerise, black, purple, soft brown, red, green, orange, pale yellow, lemon, shot-lemon, white, yellow and reddish-brown combinations, sparkling and scintillating materials.

Venus: yellow, pale blue, pastel shades, turquoise; also, white, clear blue, sky-blue to green, clear green, lemon-yellow, primrose, indigo, pink, carmine, mauve, purple, sometimes crimson and scarlet.

Mars: red, scarlet, carmine, crimson; also, claret, deep orange, pink, cerise, cherry, magenta, all angry shades, drab colours such as nondescript browns and greens.

Jupiter: blue, purple, violet; also, mixtures of red and indigo, red mixed with green, green, yellow, soft lavender, mauve, cobalt, pale lilac.

Saturn: indigo, black, greys, dark brown; also, dark blues, dark mottled shades, lead colour, purple, sage green.

Uranus: deep rich blue, checks, streaked and mixed colours; also, plaids, tartans, stripes, mingled shades, changeable colours, electric tones, silvery-white, dazzling white, mixtures of black and white, greys, violet, peacock, electric-blue, light azure, orange, banded and checked and striped blends of yellow and red and brown.

Neptune: indigo, mauve, lavender; also, pastel shades, heliotrope, grey, buff, fawn, white, black, deep blood-red, burnt umber, burnt sienna, lilac, lemon, yellow, gold, intensified turquoise, iridescence, pale greens, misty shades, deep sea-greens, colours of the ocean.

Pluto: no specific agreement among astrologers: dark red, deep fiery-green, possibly black, ultra-violet, deep crimson.

For those interested in the occult viewpoint, the *Secret Doctrine* gives: Sun (orange), Moon (violet), Mercury (yellow), Venus (indigo), Mars (red), Jupiter (blue or purple), Saturn (green).

APPENDIX IV
Metals, Minerals

The following have been gathered from a very large number of astrological writings, and from other sources.

Sun: all writers agree on gold.
Moon: silver; also, aluminium.
Mercury: Mercury, quicksilver; also, liquid metal, all alloys.
Venus: Copper; also, bronze, brass.
Mars: Iron; also, antimony, arsenic, brimstone, ochre, sulphur, vermilion, trap rocks, cinnabar.
Jupiter: all writers agree on tin.
Saturn: lead; also, coals, the dross of metals.
Uranus: uranium, radium; also, electrum, platinum, aluminium, radio-active elements.
Neptune: uncertainty among all writers. Suggestions: plastics, neptunium, platinum.
Pluto: Plutonium?

Manly Palmer Hall in his *Astrological Key Words*, presents another table of correlations with the planets which he says "may be termed the table of METALLIC AND MINERAL QUALITIES:"

Sun: glistening substances to which light seems intrinsic.
Moon: soft, smooth substances.
Mercury: flowing and veined substances.
Venus: Substances which reflect and take a high polish.
Mars: sparkling and fiery substances.
Jupiter: common and useful substances.
Saturn: dull and heavy substances, and drosses.
Uranus: electric and magnetic substances.
Neptune: dark and mysterious substances which defy analysis.

APPENDIX V

Precious Stones

The following have been gathered from a very large number of astrological writings, and from other sources. As with the correlation with the planets of colours, metals and minerals, and other matters, I personally think it doubtful whether much of the information that has been given is likely to be proven valid or, for that matter, of any particular value. However, the information derives from sincere sources and is offered to the reader in much the same spirit.

Sun: carbuncle, hyacinth, diamond, ruby, cat's-eye, chrysolite.

Moon: moonstone, selenite, pearls, opals, emerald, aquamarines, glassware, marcassite, various crystals, all soft stones.

Mercury: topaz, agate, firestone, aquamarine, glass, stones of mixed colours, liquid metal, cornelian, garnet, marble.

Venus: cornelian, alabaster, white and red coral, the beryl, chrysolite, lapis lazuli, all white stones, diamond, turquoise, sapphires of all blue shades, emerald, chrysoprasus, moss-agate, jade.

Mars: bloodstone, jasper, lodestone, red coral, ruby, flint, red garnet, malachite, sometimes the diamond.

Jupiter: amethyst, topaz, emerald, sapphire, marble, hyacinth, moonstone, carbuncle.

Saturn: toadstone, sapphire, lapis lazuli; stones of the "black, sad and ashy colour, unpolishable and ugly"; jet, and all "worthless stones in general"; galena.

Uranus: amber, and to some degree the stones connected with the Sun and Venus.

Neptune: beryl, ivory, to some degree the stones connected with the Moon and Mercury.

APPENDIX VI

The Animal Kingdom

I have collected the following assortment of animals, birds, fishes and reptiles classified under the respective planet they are said to be associated with, from a large number of sources, astrological and otherwise. Several derive from myths where they were associated with the Sun, Moon or a planet, and some were a specially choice sacrifice to the god bearing a planetary name. It will be noticed that some creatures are connected with more than one planet—the eagle, for instance—which is listed under the Sun, Mars and Jupiter.

Sun: eagle, horse, cock, lion, firefly, lynx, peacock, starfish, boar, lark, swan, nightingale, falcon, the cat and all feline animals.

Moon: bull, ox, cow, horse, crab, frog, geese, ducks, chicken, otter, owl, oyster, rabbit, sea-fowls, shell-fish, shrimps, snails, tortoise, turtle, dog, cat, mouse, pig, all amphibious creatures.

Mercury: ant, bee, fox, greyhound, hare, monkey, parrot, ape, squirrel, weasel, hyena, spider, mullet, nightingale, blackbird, swallow, jay, jackdaw, all 'swift reptiles''.

Venus: sparrow, dove, swan, swallow, deer, dolphin, partridge, pheasant, rabbit, thrush, goat, panther, wren, peacock, bee, butterfly, kingfisher, turtledove, lobster, salmon.

Mars: woodpecker, crow, eagle, hawk, panther, scorpion, tiger, vulture, fox, wolf, mastiff, kite, raven, rodents, spiders, shark, all birds and beasts of prey, all poisonous snakes and insects.

Jupiter: elephant, deer, horse, whale, ox, stag, dolphin, eagle, all domestic animals, peacock, pheasant.

Saturn: eels, shell-fish, bat, owl, cat, ass, hare, mole, mice, wolf, bear, crocodile, goat, camel, donkey, tortoise, rat, stork, beetles, crane, pelican, lion, all serpents and venomous creatures.

Uranus and Pluto: no connections found.

Neptune: horse, bull, wild boar, ram, dolphin.

APPENDIX VII

Days of the Week

The names of the days of the week can be traced back to the planetary gods after whom they were named.

Sunday (☉)
German:	*Sonntag*
Italian:	*Domenica*
French:	*Dimanche*
Anglo-Saxon:	*Sunnandæg*

Monday (☽)
German:	*Montag*
Italian:	*Lunedi*
French:	*Lundi*
Anglo-Saxon:	*Monandæg*

Tuesday (♂)
German:	*Dienstag*
Italian:	*Martedi*
French:	*Mardi*
Anglo-Saxon:	*Tiwesdæg* (Tiw)

Wednesday (☿)
German:	*Mittwoch*
Italian:	*Mercoledi*
French:	*Mercredi*
Anglo-Saxon:	*Wodneesdæg* (Woden)

Thursday (♃)
German:	*Donnerstag*
Italian:	*Giovedi*
French:	*Jeudi*
Anglo-Saxon:	*Thuresdæg* (Thor)

Friday (♀)
German:	*Freitag*
Italian:	*Venerdi*
French:	*Vendredi*
Anglo-Saxon:	*Frigedæg* (Frigga)

Saturday (♄)
German:	*Sonnabend*
Italian:	*Sabato*
French:	*Samedi*
Anglo-Saxon:	*Saeternesdæg*

APPENDIX VIII

Form and Flavour

In his *Manual of Astrology*, Sepharial proposed particular form arrangements and flavours as being connected with given planets. Theoretically, on reading through these, the reader will probably agree that the connections are ideal. But I very much doubt whether any would prove to be valid. One has only to ask oneself, "Why *should* irregular curves and crooked lines be anything at all to do with the Moon? Or, how can *all* sweet and pungent flavours be associated with the Sun? What's the point, anyway?" What *is* the point of me including these classifications in this book? Maybe it is to remind us all that a colossal amount of time has been given over to such theorizing on matters that are surely irrelevant, anyway, and far better if the theorizing had been directed to establishing psychological factors that one can interpret from a chart. Better still, if we can devote more time to establishing astrological concepts through sound research ventures and statistical testing.

The Planets and Form (according to Sepharial)

Sun: regular circles, full curves.
Moon: irregular curves, crooked lines.
Mercury: short incisive lines, slender curves.
Venus: curved lines, rhythmic scrolls.
Mars: sharp angles and barbs; pointed, fine straight lines.
Jupiter: full, generous curves.
Saturn: hard, clear-cut outlines; straight short lines; cramped forms.
Uranus: broken lines, mixed forms.
Neptune: rhythmic curves; curved lines; nebulous and chaotic forms.

The Planets and Flavour (according to Sepharial)
Sun: sweet and pungent.
Moon: insipid and odourless.
Mercury: mildly astringent and cold.
Venus: sweet and warm.
Mars: hot acids, pungent odours, burning astringents.
Jupiter: sweet and fragrant.
Saturn: cold, astringent, and sour.
Uranus: cold, astringent, brackish.
Neptune: sweet, subtile, seductive.

Index

(Note: to avoid considerably overloading the Index the names of deities, and the vast number of factors listed under the following sections have not been included here: physiological, anatomical, diseases, vegetation, vocations, colours, metals, minerals, precious stones, the animal kingdom, days of the week, form and flavour.)

C·R·C·S BOOKS

EX & THE ZODIAC: An Astrological Guide to Intimate Relationships by Helen Terrell $8.95, 256 pages. Goes into great detail in describing and analyzing the dominant traits and needs of women and men as indicated by their Zodiacal signs.

SPIRAL OF LIFE: Unlocking Your Potential with Astrology by Joanne Wickenburg & Virginia Meyer $7.95. Covering all astrological factors, this book shows how understanding the birth pattern is an exciting path toward increased self-awareness.

SPIRITUAL APPROACH TO ASTROLOGY by Myrna Lofthus $14.95, 444 pages. A complete astrology textbook from a karmic viewpoint, with an especially valuable 130-page section on karmic interpretation of all aspects, including the Ascendant & MC.

OUR SECRET SELF: Illuminating the Mysteries of the Twelfth House by Tracy Marks A Guide to Using Astrology & Your Dreams for Personal Growth. $12.95. This important book demonstrates how working with dreams is one of the most effective gateways into the hidden meanings of the Twelfth House.

CHINESE VEGETARIAN COOKERY by Jack Santa Maria $7.95. *VEGETARIAN* magazine called this "the best" of all the books on Chinese vegetarian cookery. It is by far the most accessible for Westerners and uses ingredients that are easily found anywhere.

THE FOOD ALLERGY PLAN: A Working Doctor's Self-Help Guide to New Medical Discoveries by Keith Mumby $7.95. A step-by-step guide that helps the reader identify and eliminate those foods which cause anxiety, irritation, or symptoms of illness.

HEALTH BUILDING: The Conscious Art of Living Well by Dr. Randolph Stone $9.95. A complete health program for people of all ages, based on vital energy currents. Includes instructions on vegetarian & purifying diets and energizing exercises for vitality & beauty.

HELPING YOURSELF WITH NATURAL REMEDIES: An Encyclopedic Guide to Herbal & Nutritional Treatment by Terry Willard, Ph.D. $12.95. This easily accessible book blends 20th century scientific & clinical experience with traditional methods of health maintenance. Allows you to select natural remedies for over 100 specific problems, all arranged in alphabetical order & with a complete index.

MATCHING GOOD HEALTH WITH HOMEOPATHIC MEDICINE: A Concise, Self-Help Introduction to Homeopathy by Raymond J. Garrett & TaRessa Stone $7.95. Includes dozens of fascinating personal stories of striking cures, as well as guidelines to choosing effective remedies for first-aid and sports injuries.

POLARITY THERAPY: VOL. I & II: The Complete Collected Works by Dr. Randolph Stone, D.O., D.C. $25.00 each. The original books on this revolutionary healing art, available for the first time in trade editions. Fully illustrated with charts & diagrams. Sewn binding.

PROTEIN-BALANCED VEGETARIAN COOKERY by David Scott $8.95, 184 pages. The only cookbook that focuses on the crucial issue of protein balance and protein-sufficiency.

TAI CHI: TEN MINUTES TO HEALTH: The Most Comprehensive Guide to Yang Tai Chi by Chia Siew Pang & Goh Ewe Hock $16.95, 132 pages. The most comprehensive manual on Yang style Tai Chi available, which breaks down the movements in more detail than any other book. Recommended by American Library Association's "Booklist."

YOGA FOR THE WEST: A Manual for Designing Your Own Practice by Ian Rawlinson $17.95. A large-size, profusely illustrated paperback with a sewn binding that opens flat for easy use, this pioneering book provides Western students of Yoga with a guide to adapting the ancient principles to the modern person's needs.

For more complete information on our books, a complete catalog, or to order any of the above publications, WRITE TO:

CRCS Publications
Post Office Box 1460
Sebastopol, California 95473
U.S.A.

ASTROLOGY, PSYCHOLOGY,
AND
THE FOUR ELEMENTS

An Energy Approach to Astrology &
Its Use in the Counseling Arts

Stephen Arroyo

This book deals with the relation of astrology to modern psychology and with the use of astrology as a practical method of understanding one's attunement to universal forces. It clearly shows how to approach astrology with a real understanding of the energies involved, and it includes practical instruction in the interpretation of astrological factors with more depth than is commonly found in astrological textbooks. Part I was awarded the 1973 Astrology Prize by the British Astrological Association as the most valuable contribution to astrology during that year.

PART I: ASTROLOGY & PSYCHOLOGY

Part I thoroughly explains how astrology can be the most valuable psychological tool for understanding oneself and others. Analyzing the scientific, philosophical, and intuitive dimensions of astrology, it is oriented toward the layman with no astrological knowledge, astrology students and professionals, and those engaged in any form of the counseling arts.

PART II: THE FOUR ELEMENTS
AN ENERGY APPROACH TO INTERPRETING
BIRTH-CHARTS

Part II deals specifically with the interpretation and practical application of astrological factors based on the actual energies involved (air, fire, water, & earth). It presents a dynamic application of astrological knowledge that clarifies and illuminates traditional techniques and meanings by placing them in the perspective of understanding the vital energies inherent in all life processes.

From:

_____

_____

_____

I am interested in books on the following subjects & would like to receive a catalogue of your titles.

☐ Vegetarian Cookery
☐ Holistic Health & Natural Healing
☐ Astrology

To:

CRCS Publications
P. O. Box 1460
Sebastopol, CA 95473
U.S.A.

ORDER FORM

Holistic Health

☐ Chinese Vegetarian Cookery by Jack Santa Maria $ 7.95 _____

☐ The Food Allergy Plan: A Working Doctor's Self-Help $ 7.95 _____
  Guide to New Medical Discoveries by Dr. Keith Mumby

☐ Health Building: The Conscious Art of Living Well by Dr. Randolph Stone $ 8.95 _____

☐ Helping Yourself With Natural Remedies: An Encyclopedic Guide to $12.95 _____
  Herbal & Nutritional Treatment by Terry Willard, Ph.D.

☐ Polarity Therapy: The Complete Collected Works by Dr. Randolph Stone $25.ea. _____
  (Vols. I & II)

☐ Protein-Balanced Vegetarian Cookery by David Scott $ 8.95 _____

☐ Tai Chi: Ten Minutes to Health: The Most Comprehensive Guide to Tai   15.95 _____
  Chi by Pang & Hock. 800 illus.

☐ Yoga for the West: A Manual for Designing Your Own Practice by $17.95 _____
  Ian Rawlinson

Astrology

☐ The Ancient Science of Geomancy: Living in Harmony with the Earth $12.95 _____
  by Nigel Pennick

☐ The Art of Chart Interpretation by Tracy Marks. A Step-by-Step Method $ 7.95 _____

☐ The Astrologer's Manual: Modern Insights into an Ancient Art by $10.95 _____
  Landis Knight Green

☐ The Astrological Houses: The Spectrum of Individual Experience by $ 8.95 _____
  Dane Rudhyar

☐ Astrology: The Classic Guide to Understanding Your Horoscope by $ 8.95 _____
  Ronald C. Davison

☐ Astrology in Modern Language by Richard Vaughan. Focuses on the $12.95 _____
  Houses & Ruling Planets

☐ Astrology, Karma & Transformation: The Inner Dimensions of the Birth $12.95 _____
  Chart by Stephen Arroyo. An international best-seller!

☐ Astrology of Self-Discovery by Tracy Marks. Emphasizes Neptune, Pluto $10.95 _____
  & the Moon

☐ Astrology, Psychology & The Four Elements by Stephen Arroyo. A $ 9.95 _____
  Modern Classic!

☐ Stephen Arroyo's Chart Interpretation Handbook: Guidelines for Under- $ 8.95 _____
  standing the Essentials of the Birth Chart

☐ Planetary Aspects: How to Make Your Stressful Aspects Work for You by $11.95 _____
  Tracy Marks

☐ Reincarnation Through the Zodiac by Joan Hodgson $ 6.95 _____

☐ Relationships & Life Cycles: Modern Dimensions of Astrology by $ 8.95 _____
  Stephen Arroyo

☐ Sex & The Zodiac: An Astrological Guide to Intimate Relationships by $ 7.95 _____
  Helen Terrell

☐ A Spiritual Approach to Astrology: A Complete Textbook of Astrology by $12.95 _____
  M. Lofthus

☐ Your Secret Self: Illuminating the Mysteries of the Twelfth House by $12.95 _____
  Tracy Marks

☐ Astrology in Action: How Astrology Works in Practice by Paul Wright $12.95 _____

☐ The Jupiter/Saturn Conference Lectures by Stephen Arroyo & Lize Greene $ 8.95 _____

Please note: Free shipping on orders over $35.00. Add $1.75 postage on smaller orders.
*Foreign customers please send funds in U.S. dollars.

Subtotal: _____

+ 6% tax (Calif. Residents): _____

Add $1.75 postage if order $35. or less: _____

Enclose payment in an envelope addressed to:
CRCS Publications, P.O. Box 1460, Sebastopol, CA 95473

*TOTAL: _____

Name: _____

Address: _____

City: _____ State: _____

Zip: _____ COUNTRY: _____

PLEASE PRINT CLEARLY OR TYPE!!   *Thank you for your interest in our books*